LÉON BLUM

LÉON BLUM

Stephen Eric Bronner

Rutgers University

1987
CHELSEA HOUSE PUBLISHERS
NEW YORK
NEW HAVEN   PHILADELPHIA

EDITORIAL DIRECTOR: Nancy Toff
MANAGING EDITOR: Karyn Gullen Browne
COPY CHIEF: Perry Scott King
ART DIRECTOR: Giannella Garrett
ASSISTANT ART DIRECTOR: Carol McDougall
PICTURE EDITOR: Elizabeth Terhune

Staff for LÉON BLUM:

SENIOR EDITOR: John W. Selfridge
ASSISTANT EDITORS: Maria Behan, Pierre Hauser, Howard Ratner, Bert Yaeger
COPY EDITORS: Sean Dolan, Kathleen McDermott
ASSISTANT DESIGNER: Noreen Lamb
PICTURE RESEARCH: Matthew Miller, Juliette Dickstein
LAYOUT: Kingsley Parker
PRODUCTION COORDINATOR: Alma Rodriguez
PRODUCTION ASSISTANT: Karen Dreste
COVER ILLUSTRATION: Robin Peterson

CREATIVE DIRECTOR: Harold Steinberg

Frontispiece courtesy of AP/Wide World Photos

First Printing

Library of Congress Cataloging in Publication Data

Bronner, Stephen. LÉON BLUM

(World leaders past & present)
Bibliography: p.
Includes index.
1. Blum, Léon, 1872–1950— Juvenile literature.
2. Statesmen—France—Biography— Juvenile literature.
3. France—Politics and government—20th century—
Juvenile literature. [1. Blum, Léon, 1872–1950.
2. Statesmen] I. Title. II. Series.
DC373.B5B76   1986   944.081'5'0924 [B] [92]   86-13710

ISBN 0-87754-511-1

Contents

CHELSEA HOUSE PUBLISHERS

WORLD LEADERS PAST & PRESENT

ON LEADERSHIP
Arthur M. Schlesinger, jr.

LEADERSHIP, it may be said, is really what makes the world go round. Love no doubt smooths the passage; but love is a private transaction between consenting adults. Leadership is a public transaction with history. The idea of leadership affirms the capacity of individuals to move, inspire, and mobilize masses of people so that they act together in pursuit of an end. Sometimes leadership serves good purposes, sometimes bad; but whether the end is benign or evil, great leaders are those men and women who leave their personal stamp on history.

Now, the very concept of leadership implies the proposition that individuals can make a difference. This proposition has never been universally accepted. From classical times to the present day, eminent thinkers have regarded individuals as no more than the agents and pawns of larger forces, whether the gods and goddesses of the ancient world or, in the modern era, race, class, nation, the dialectic, the will of the people, the spirit of the times, history itself. Against such forces, the individual dwindles into insignificance.

So contends the thesis of historical determinism. Tolstoy's great novel *War and Peace* offers a famous statement of the case. Why, Tolstoy asked, did millions of men in the Napoleonic wars, denying their human feelings and their common sense, move back and forth across Europe slaughtering their fellows? "The war," Tolstoy answered, "was bound to happen simply because it was bound to happen." All prior history predetermined it. As for leaders, they, Tolstoy said, "are but the labels that serve to give a name to an end and, like labels, they have the least possible connection with the event." The greater the leader, "the more conspicuous the inevitability and the predestination of every act he commits." The leader, said Tolstoy, is "the slave of history."

Determinism takes many forms. Marxism is the determinism of class. Nazism the determinism of race. But the idea of men and women as the slaves of history runs athwart the deepest human instincts. Rigid determinism abolishes the idea of human freedom—

the assumption of free choice that underlies every move we make, every word we speak, every thought we think. It abolishes the idea of human responsibility, since it is manifestly unfair to reward or punish people for actions that are by definition beyond their control. No one can live consistently by any deterministic creed. The Marxist states prove this themselves by their extreme susceptibility to the cult of leadership.

More than that, history refutes the idea that individuals make no difference. In December 1931 a British politician crossing Park Avenue in New York City between 76th and 77th Streets around 10:30 P.M. looked in the wrong direction and was knocked down by an automobile—a moment, he later recalled, of a man aghast, a world aglare: "I do not understand why I was not broken like an eggshell or squashed like a gooseberry." Fourteen months later an American politician, sitting in an open car in Miami, Florida, was fired on by an assassin; the man beside him was hit. Those who believe that individuals make no difference to history might well ponder whether the next two decades would have been the same had Mario Constasino's car killed Winston Churchill in 1931 and Giuseppe Zangara's bullet killed Franklin Roosevelt in 1933. Suppose, in addition, that Adolf Hitler had been killed in the street fighting during the Munich *Putsch* of 1923 and that Lenin had died of typhus during World War I. What would the 20th century be like now?

For better or for worse, individuals do make a difference. "The notion that a people can run itself and its affairs anonymously," wrote the philosopher William James, "is now well known to be the silliest of absurdities. Mankind does nothing save through initiatives on the part of inventors, great or small, and imitation by the rest of us—these are the sole factors in human progress. Individuals of genius show the way, and set the patterns, which common people then adopt and follow."

Leadership, James suggests, means leadership in thought as well as in action. In the long run, leaders in thought may well make the greater difference to the world. But, as Woodrow Wilson once said, "Those only are leaders of men, in the general eye, who lead in action. . . . It is at their hands that new thought gets its translation into the crude language of deeds." Leaders in thought often invent in solitude and obscurity, leaving to later generations the tasks of imitation. Leaders in action—the leaders portrayed in this series—have to be effective in their own time.

And they cannot be effective by themselves. They must act in response to the rhythms of their age. Their genius must be adapted, in a phrase of William James's, "to the receptivities of the moment." Leaders are useless without followers. "There goes the mob," said the French politician hearing a clamor in the streets. "I am their leader. I must follow them." Great leaders turn the inchoate emotions of the mob to purposes of their own. They seize on the opportunities of their time, the hopes, fears, frustrations, crises, potentialities. They succeed when events have prepared the way for them, when the community is awaiting to be aroused, when they can provide the clarifying and organizing ideas. Leadership ignites the circuit between the individual and the mass and thereby alters history.

It may alter history for better or for worse. Leaders have been responsible for the most extravagant follies and most monstrous crimes that have beset suffering humanity. They have also been vital in such gains as humanity has made in individual freedom, religious and racial tolerance, social justice and respect for human rights.

There is no sure way to tell in advance who is going to lead for good and who for evil. But a glance at the gallery of men and women in *World Leaders—Past and Present* suggests some useful tests.

One test is this: do leaders lead by force or by persuasion? By command or by consent? Through most of history leadership was exercised by the divine right of authority. The duty of followers was to defer and to obey. "Theirs not to reason why,/ Theirs but to do and die." On occasion, as with the so-called "enlightened despots" of the 18th century in Europe, absolutist leadership was animated by humane purposes. More often, absolutism nourished the passion for domination, land, gold and conquest and resulted in tyranny.

The great revolution of modern times has been the revolution of equality. The idea that all people should be equal in their legal condition has undermined the old structure of authority, hierarchy and deference. The revolution of equality has had two contrary effects on the nature of leadership. For equality, as Alexis de Tocqueville pointed out in his great study *Democracy in America*, might mean equality in servitude as well as equality in freedom.

"I know of only two methods of establishing equality in the political world," Tocqueville wrote. "Rights must be given to every citizen, or none at all to anyone . . . save one, who is the master of all." There was no middle ground "between the sovereignty of all and the absolute power of one man." In his astonishing prediction of 20th-century totalitarian dictatorship, Tocqueville explained how the revolution of equality could lead to the *"Führerprinzip"* and more terrible absolutism than the world had ever known.

But when rights are given to every citizen and the sovereignty of all is established, the problem of leadership takes a new form, becomes more exacting than ever before. It is easy to issue commands and enforce them by the rope and the stake, the concentration camp and the *gulag.* It is much harder to use argument and achievement to overcome opposition and win consent. The Founding Fathers of the United States understood the difficulty. They believed that history had given them the opportunity to decide, as Alexander Hamilton wrote in the first Federalist Paper, whether men are indeed capable of basing government on "reflection and choice, or whether they are forever destined to depend . . . on accident and force."

Government by reflection and choice called for a new style of leadership and a new quality of followership. It required leaders to be responsive to popular concerns, and it required followers to be active and informed participants in the process. Democracy does not eliminate emotion from politics; sometimes it fosters demagoguery; but it is confident that, as the greatest of democratic leaders put it, you cannot fool all of the people all of the time. It measures leadership by results and retires those who overreach or falter or fail.

It is true that in the long run despots are measured by results too. But they can postpone the day of judgment, sometimes indefinitely, and in the meantime they can do infinite harm. It is also true that democracy is no guarantee of virtue and intelligence in government, for the voice of the people is not necessarily the voice of God. But democracy, by assuring the right of opposition, offers built-in resistance to the evils inherent in absolutism. As the theologian Reinhold Niebuhr summed it up, "Man's capacity for justice makes democracy possible, but man's inclination to injustice makes democracy necessary."

A second test for leadership is the end for which power is sought. When leaders have as their goal the supremacy of a master race or the promotion of totalitarian revolution or the acquisition and exploitation of colonies or the protection of greed and privilege or the preservation of personal power, it is likely that their leadership will do little to advance the cause of humanity. When their goal is the abolition of slavery, the liberation of women, the enlargement of opportunity for the poor and powerless, the extension of equal rights to racial minorities, the defense of the freedoms of expression and opposition, it is likely that their leadership will increase the sum of human liberty and welfare.

Leaders have done great harm to the world. They have also conferred great benefits. You will find both sorts in this series. Even "good" leaders must be regarded with a certain wariness. Leaders are not demigods; they put on their trousers one leg after another just like ordinary mortals. No leader is infallible, and every leader needs to be reminded of this at regular intervals. Irreverence irritates leaders but is their salvation. Unquestioning submission corrupts leaders and demands followers. Making a cult of a leader is always a mistake. Fortunately hero worship generates its own antidote. "Every hero," said Emerson, "becomes a bore at last."

The signal benefit the great leaders confer is to embolden the rest of us to live according to our own best selves, to be active, insistent, and resolute in affirming our own sense of things. For great leaders attest to the reality of human freedom against the supposed inevitabilities of history. And they attest to the wisdom and power that may lie within the most unlikely of us, which is why Abraham Lincoln remains the supreme example of great leadership. A great leader, said Emerson, exhibits new possibilities to all humanity. "We feed on genius. . . . Great men exist that there may be greater men."

Great leaders, in short, justify themselves by emancipating and empowering their followers. So humanity struggles to master its destiny, remembering with Alexis de Tocqueville: "It is true that around every man a fatal circle is traced beyond which he cannot pass; but within the wide verge of that circle he is powerful and free; as it is with man, so with communities."

—*New York*

11

1

The Making of a Socialist

The afternoon of February 13, 1936, found Léon Blum lying wounded in a hospital bed. That morning he had been driven down a street where a demonstration was in progress. The rally's participants opposed France's parliamentary democratic system, with its numerous political parties and civil liberties. They were "fascists," men and women of right-wing political views, who believed that democracy had produced an excess of factional conflict, rule by the "rabble," constant economic crises that benefited "Jewish" financiers, and a loss of traditional values.

The protesters looked with admiration to Italy and Germany. In those countries, Benito Mussolini and Adolf Hitler had created "totalitarian" dictatorships, seeming prosperity, and a fresh sense of purpose with their programs of racial hatred and simple-minded nationalism. The demonstrators longed for France to rally around a slogan like that of the German Nazis: "One People! One Leader! One Nation!"

The crowd was large and angry. As the car inched forward, someone recognized the famous man inside. Cries for blood arose instantly. It was as if Léon

In critical times men can save their lives only by risking them.
—LÉON BLUM

The face of Léon Blum, characterized by spectacles and thick mustache, became well-known throughout France during the first half of the 20th century. Throughout his long career as a writer, lawyer, critic, politician, and head of three governments, Léon Blum was to suffer vicious slanders, mockery, even imprisonment, to emerge finally as a hero of socialist France.

13

Severely injured, Blum recuperates in a hospital ward. On February 13, 1936, Blum's party had mistakenly driven into the middle of a radical rightist, Action Française funeral parade. Yelling "death to the Jew," the crowd had dragged Blum from the car and beaten him almost to death.

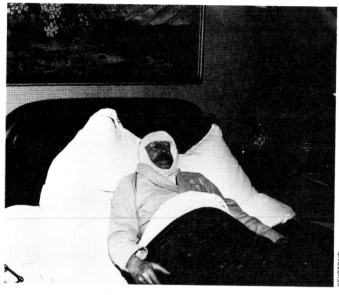

KEYSTONE

> *Socialism is born of the concern for human equality because the society in which we live is founded on privilege. It is born of the pity and anger that is aroused in every honest heart by the intolerable spectacle of poverty, unemployment, cold, and hunger. It is born of the contrast, scandalous and heart-rending, between the luxury of some and the privation of others, between crushing toil and insolent idleness.*
>
> —LÉON BLUM

Blum embodied everything that the mob held in contempt. He was a Jew who had attended the best schools and who was admitted to elite circles. He was a literary man and a cultivated, worldly intellectual. He was a refined speaker who inspired his audiences. Above all, Blum was the acknowledged leader of France's socialist movement, an ardent democrat, and a tireless worker in the French struggle against fascism.

An election was soon to take place, pitting the conservative and fascist parties of the Right against a coalition of left-wing parties known as the Popular Front. The demonstrators knew that the Popular Front would be led by Blum's large socialist party, which sought radical social and economic reforms to insure a more equitable distribution of wealth. They also understood that this Popular Front included the French Communist party, which was loyal to the policies of the Soviet Union, as well as the liberal Radical party, which supported the French republic along with its existing capitalist economic system. The very future of France seemed to hang in the balance and the choice was clear: fascism or democracy. As far as the demonstrators were concerned, "Better Hitler than Blum!"

The mob circled the car, pounded it from all sides, rocked it back and forth. Blum was dragged from the car, insulted, spat upon, and beaten. His two companions, the socialist parliamentary deputy Georges Monnet and his wife, along with a passerby and two policemen, cleared a space and placed him on the ground. Luckily, some construction workers nearby noticed what was happening. They made their way to the embattled little group and carried away Blum, who was unconscious and bleeding profusely. He was 63 years old.

Even before this attack in 1936, Blum's political life had been marked by trying periods. He had witnessed the horrors of World War I, the rise of communism and fascism, the murder of friends, as well as the enormous suffering and unemployment caused by the world economic depression of 1929. As a Jew, he had suffered particular anguish over the growth of anti-Semitism in Europe. Soon enough he would experience the outbreak of a second world war. Following the fall of France to Nazi armies in June 1940, he would stand trial for treason and ultimately find himself deported to a German concentration camp. Still, the old man would survive and, upon the Nazi defeat, return to France in glory.

A huge crowd of leftist Parisians fills the Boulevard St. Germain. Headed by the leadership of the Popular Front coalition, more than a half million demonstrators marched across the city in protest of the attack on their leader, Léon Blum, on this street three days before.

Young Léon Blum (second from right) with his four brothers. The boys were raised in a wealthy Jewish family where education was greatly cherished.

Léon with his mother. Marie Blum had a profound influence on her son, transmitting to him what he later called "an intensity of scruples": a deep commitment to justice that would remain the theme of Blum's life work.

It is, however, that image of Léon Blum under assault from the Right, defending the principles of democracy and socialism, that in large part defines his place in history. Three days after the riot, a much larger leftist demonstration took place. It was called to protest the violent attack on the socialist leader and seemed to provide a prophecy. For, in the spring of 1936, the Popular Front took power and Léon Blum became premier of France. It was the first administration in French history to be led by socialists.

The Popular Front would temporarily unify the Left, forestall the rise of fascism in France, and pass a set of radical economic measures to better the lives of working people. In a way, this political experiment was a great success; in another way, it was a tragic failure. Nevertheless, the Popular Front would ultimately serve the future as a true symbol for the spirit of hope and the cause of freedom.

Léon Blum was born in Paris on April 9, 1872, one of five children in a prosperous Jewish household. His parents, Abraham and Marie Blum, were basically nonreligious and open-minded people who valued learning and a personal commitment to justice. Blum's mother had an especially strong influence on him. In the Europe of that time, many Jewish, middle-class families tended to embrace the democratic values generated by the French Revolution of 1789, with its great slogan, "Liberty, Equality, and Fraternity."

Léon showed remarkable intellectual gifts at a very young age, and he was therefore able to attend the most prestigious high school in Paris. Afterward he was admitted to France's most time-honored academic institution, the École Normale Supérieure, from which the country historically chose its political and intellectual leaders. At the age of 19, he withdrew from the École Normale and enrolled simultaneously in the Faculty of Letters and the Faculty of Law at the Sorbonne, France's most prestigious university. Very early on, Blum became interested in literature and gained considerable fame as a writer and critic. It was during these early years

that he made friends with many people who would later comprise France's cultural elite. It was also during these years that he first became involved with politics and socialism.

When Blum was a student entering his twenties, Paris had become the acknowledged center of world culture. The Eiffel Tower had just been erected, and the city had recently been redesigned to give it a more modern look. Despite the dire poverty of the working masses and the instability of France's Third Republic (founded in 1871), a sense of optimism prevailed, particularly among industrialists

The Eiffel Tower dominates a view of the Centennial Exposition of 1889. Symbolizing the principles of the French Revolution, 100 years before, the structure was a constant reminder to the French of their victory over oppressive governments.

and businessmen. Indeed, the years in which Blum grew to maturity would come to be known as *la belle époque* (the beautiful epoch).

Behind the glittering façade of the upper classes, however, profound currents of discontent and a cultural rebellion were taking shape. Young nonconformists were appalled by what they saw as an impoverishment of spiritual life and by French society's seemingly all-consuming passion for money. They believed that human sensibility and individuality were threatened by the growth of heavy industry, the spread of governmental bureaucracy, and the rise of a uniform "mass culture." Above all, however, these rebels despised their establishment's "Victorianism," with its moralistic attitudes, conservative customs, and repressive sexual values.

In cafés and taverns, living rooms and attics, artists, bohemians, and intellectuals of different political views came together. Circles formed, journals appeared, exhibitions took place, with varying degrees of influence on French culture. The participants read one another's works, heard one

A Paris salon in 1901. Salons were a cultural tradition in France where intellectuals gathered to discuss the issues of the day. The stylish, cultured Blum was welcome in the elite salons of Paris, and it was at such places where he learned of liberal issues and the precepts of socialism.

another's concerts, saw one another's paintings, and endlessly debated political and cultural issues. In this stimulating environment, Blum encountered the future.

From old, rich families came young writers like Marcel Proust, who would later publish *Remembrance of Things Past*, one of the greatest 20th-century novels, and André Gide, who would become a world-famous man of letters and a Nobel Prize winner. There were major artists like Henri de Toulouse-Lautrec, whose paintings were called "frescoes of the poor." Then there were important composers like the embittered Claude Debussy, and angry experimental poets like Paul Verlaine and Guillaume Apollinaire. All would figure prominently in the history of modern culture.

The views of these bohemians covered the entire political spectrum. The Right may have been elitist, antidemocratic, and even anti-intellectual, but it never lacked artists and writers. Gide and Proust both flirted with the Right. This was also the case with the great impressionist painter Edgar Degas and the extraordinary poet Paul Claudel. Along with intellectual charlatans like Paul Bourget and Charles Maurras, who would later become *the* thinker of the powerful fascist movement Action Française (French Action), the Right included some remarkable talents.

Still, the writers of the Left exerted the greatest influence on Blum. They were committed to democracy and equality, to reason and the free play of ideas, to social justice and tolerance. The novelist Anatole France was a popular proponent of such principles, as was the courageous publicist and publisher Georges Clemenceau (though he would abandon the values of the Left once he became premier and virtual dictator of France during World War I), and Henri Barbusse, the future pacifist and communist spokesperson for the Popular Front. Finally, there was Émile Zola, a true crusader for social justice, who caused one scandal after another with novels like *Nana* and *Germinal*, which exposed the hidden cruelty and exploitative character of French society.

> *Every individual has a right to demand of humanity everything that will aid his effort; he has the right to work, to produce, to create; and no category of man may draw usury from his work or put it under its yoke.*
> — JEAN JAURÈS
> French socialist leader

Lucien Herr, librarian of École Normale Supérieure. From his post at this school for intellectual students, Herr helped mold the minds of a generation. Blum called him "my confessor, converter, guide . . . director of my conscience and my thoughts."

Two men, however, would hold a special importance for Blum's political career. While still at school, Blum met Lucien Herr, who would serve as the librarian at the École Normale from 1888 until his death in 1926. It was from this rather modest post that Herr, who wrote very little, influenced an entire generation of French intellectuals. An early supporter of the socialist cause, Herr soon became Blum's confidant, adviser, and political ally. He also introduced Blum to a true political giant, the most famous of all French socialists, who would become the most dominant influence on his political development: Jean Jaurès.

This litany of names gives a sense of the exciting cultural climate wherein Blum grew to maturity, one that deepened the young man's vision and exposed him to a broad variety of political outlooks.

Indeed, he became part of a community that, even after France's political scene became increasingly polarized, remained in many ways intact.

In 1894 Blum graduated from the Sorbonne, receiving his degree in law and literature. The next year, deeming the prospects for a literary career too uncertain, he accepted a position as a lawyer for the Conseil d'État, the highest administrative court in France and the one that hears all litigation pitting the government against private citizens. Blum would serve the court with distinction for 25 years, delivering briefs and recommendations that remain part of the permanent body of French administrative law.

Still, Blum never completely abandoned the literary life. In numerous journals like *La Revue Blanche* (*The White Review*), he published book and theater reviews, along with poetry and essays. Surely it was the freedom he experienced in his Parisian intellectual circle that inspired him to write his controversial *On Marriage*. Later, to howls of disgust from the Right, the distinguished leader of the socialist movement would republish this early work, in which he argued that a variety of premarital sexual experiences was an essential prelude to a happy marriage.

It was another work, however, that first brought Blum before a broader public. A series of philosophical, literary, and political essays, most of which were written between 1894 and 1896, it was originally published in separate parts. When the work finally appeared as a whole in 1901, it was praised by the young and derided by traditionalists. The book's breadth and sheer audacity made it unique. Indeed, *New Conversations of Goethe with Eckermann* also provides important clues to Blum's personality, values, and future political course.

The structure of the book was suggested by a 19th-century work, *Conversations with Eckermann*. This was a collection of dialogues between the world-renowned writer Johann Wolfgang von Goethe and his friend and secretary, Johann Peter Eckermann. Goethe is perhaps best known for his semiautobiographical novel of adolescence and un-

> *In difficult moments it was always from his memory and teachings that I have sought the guide to my actions. I did not ask myself: 'What would he have done in my place?' — I never had the presumption to substitute myself for him in even my thought — but I asked myself: 'What would he have wanted me to do, I such as I am?'*
> —LÉON BLUM
> describing the influence of Jean Jaurès on his life

requited love, *The Sorrows of Young Werther,* and for his later dramatic poem *Faust,* which is unquestionably one of the most magnificent achievements of world literature. Goethe was a man of tremendous scope and learning whose interests ranged from poetry and philosophy to science and politics. Even today, Goethe stands as a true symbol of reason and universal genius.

It was not exactly an act of modesty for Blum, then only 22, to modernize those wide-ranging "conversations" of the revered Goethe. No less than the original, however, Blum's work tries to cover the spectrum of modern existence. Indeed, the *New Conversations* shows Blum's remarkable mixture of intellectual and emotional self-confidence with which he later endured the flood of vicious and degrading attacks leveled by the fascist and the communist presses. The choice of Goethe as a model

Johann Wolfgang von Goethe, one of the giants of world literature. After his death, Goethe's thoughts on a range of subjects were presented in dialogue form by his friend Johann Peter Eckermann. This work served as the inspiration for Blum's controversial *New Conversations of Goethe with Eckermann,* which attempted to modernize the theories of the 18th-century scholar-philosopher.

demonstrates Blum's commitment to humanist ideals.

Though consisting of various accounts of, and observations on, aspects of everyday life, the *New Conversations* is truly inspired ethical and political philosophy. Blum praises Anatole France, Zola, Gide, and Proust over and against Maurras and Bourget. Like Goethe, the young writer mixes criticism of traditional social prejudices with a concern for democracy, equality, justice, tolerance for new ideas, the power of reason, and the dignity of the individual. The *New Conversations* glows with reverence for Goethe and great figures of the Enlightenment, such as the philosophers Voltaire and Diderot, who inspired some of the most progressive values of the French Revolution with their persuasive arguments for democratic rights and cultural freedom. Still, unlike members of the socialist movement that Blum would join in his middle twenties, they essentially ignored economic inequality and the dire plight of the impoverished masses. Consequently, in referring to those extraordinary intellectuals of the 18th century, Blum put the matter well when he said that "their eyes were not open to the obvious."

During the close of the 19th century, however, many people would dogmatically choose to close their eyes and turn their backs on every democratic ideal derived from the Enlightenment and the French Revolution. In France a bizarre and terrible conflict was beginning, the effects of which would carry over well into the 20th century. This conflict would assume such significance that governments would topple, mobs would fight, friends would become enemies, and even families would break apart. It would become impossible to remain aloof. Indeed, the Dreyfus Affair would forever create a fundamental divide between the blind and those who dared to live with their eyes open.

> *The son of a blacksmith ought to be able to become prime minister, but a prime minister's son, if he has no talent, should not expect to be more than a blacksmith.*
> —LÉON BLUM
> in *New Conversations of Goethe with Eckermann*, published in 1901

2

Justice Calls

It was only in 1935, when France once again stood divided between the Left and the Right, that Léon Blum published his *Remembrances of the Affair*. The Dreyfus Affair of the 1890s must have seemed like a dress rehearsal for the conflicts of the 1930s. No doubt, Blum felt that this crucial event from the past provided an important moral lesson.

Beyond the passions the affair originally inspired, Blum's work shows how it generated a web of intrigue and deceit. On October 15, 1894, an obscure army captain was accused of treason. An itemized list of documents supplied to Germany had been discovered a little while earlier by the counterespionage branch of the French military. Given the sensitive information the list contained, the source was obviously someone on the army general staff.

The military leadership wanted a speedy trial. The army had suffered a devastating defeat in the Franco-Prussian War of 1871 and its image remained somewhat tarnished. Since the army hoped to win increased funding from the government so that it could pursue a policy of revenge for earlier losses, it feared any possible blow to its prestige. As

Neither for my friends, nor for myself, did life count. We would have sacrificed ourselves without the slightest hesitation and without the slightest effort for what we held to be the cause of truth and justice. And undoubtedly, although with somewhat more difficulty, we would have sacrificed the men who barred the way to justice and to truth.
—LÉON BLUM
recalling, in his 1935 book
Remembrances of the Affair, his dedication to the Dreyfusard cause

Blum in his early 20s. Already an acclaimed writer, he began to study law, guaranteeing himself a more secure lifestyle. It was at this time that the Dreyfus Affair surfaced in France. In taking the case, Blum was embroiled in a volatile political situation.

A scene from France's desperate last stand in Sedan during the Franco-Prussian War. The siege ended with the capture of 83,000 French soldiers, as well as Emperor Napoleon III. In the aftermath, the democratic Third Republic was formed, bitterly hated by the remnants of the imperial army.

rumors of treason spread, the military leadership was forced to find a scapegoat. Hurriedly, on the basis of forgeries and other falsified evidence, a "traitor" was chosen — Alfred Dreyfus, the only Jew on the army general staff.

A military trial was arranged. Supposed witnesses were summoned to testify against Dreyfus. Handwriting analysts were pressured into claiming that Dreyfus was the author of the list. The real traitor, a shiftless and totally corrupt aristocrat named Major Charles-Ferdinand Esterhazy, surely breathed a sigh of relief when the verdict was given. The innocent Dreyfus was condemned and sent to the penal colony at Devil's Island in French Guyana on April 13, 1895, where, for roughly four years, he would endure terrible hardship.

At first, almost no one questioned the verdict. In openly anti-Semitic circles monarchists and nationalists applauded the verdict. Journals and organizations of the Right, like Édouard Drumont's *The Free Word* and Jules Guerin's National Anti-Semitic League, joyously proclaimed that the army had fi-

finally exposed a member of the "Jewish syndicate" — an imagined conspiracy, supposedly bent on undermining the Catholic church and overthrowing the French state.

Of course, such a syndicate never existed. But for some people the conviction of Captain Dreyfus reinforced the notion that the Jews were in the pay of Germany. Needless to say, German anti-Semites were busy proclaiming similar nonsense, but they said that the Jewish "conspiracy" was really aligned with France.

It is interesting, however, to consider the responses of other, more responsible groups to the conviction of Dreyfus. Mainstream Jewish organizations, fearful of making waves amid a growing anti-Semitism, grudgingly accepted the verdict and missed no chance to express their nationalism. Liberals and traditional conservatives simply assumed that the army was telling the truth. Though some were more skeptical, that was also the case for many socialists. Jean Jaurès, for example, originally assumed Dreyfus to be guilty. In fact, Jaurès actually demanded the death penalty for *Captain* Dreyfus since, in all fairness, a mere worker would surely have been executed for the crime.

Of course, some people were not fooled. They knew that Dreyfus was an honest man and a staunch nationalist, that he had no financial worries, and that it would have been insane for the only Jew on the army general staff to risk the office he had attained against so much prejudice. These skeptics did not believe Dreyfus had a motive for committing treason and also recognized that his military specialty made him an unlikely candidate to transmit the type of information in question. To the perceptive few, the whole trial smelled of a frame-up.

As the embers of the case continued to smolder and the Dreyfus family stood close to despair, the break finally came. The free-spending Esterhazy once again needed money, and following the conviction of Dreyfus, he resumed his treasonous activity. Early in 1896, a Colonel Georges Picquart of military intelligence intercepted a memo from Esterhazy to a German military attaché. Picquart im-

Alfred Dreyfus, the Jewish army officer falsely accused of passing military secrets to the Germans. Dreyfus was framed to deflect embarrassing criticism from the military. Forged documents were drawn up and Dreyfus was convicted. For nearly 12 years, France was divided over the demand for a retrial.

Colonel Georges Picquart, the military intelligence officer who recognized Esterhazy's handwriting on treasonous documents supposedly written by Dreyfus. His superiors ordered him to remain silent, threatening both his life and position. Unwilling to be silenced, he revealed the facts to friends, which blew open the scandal.

When truth is buried underground it grows, it chokes, it gathers such an explosive force that on the day it bursts out, it blows up everything with it.

—ÉMILE ZOLA
quoted from "J'accuse," an
exposé of the Dreyfus Affair
published in *L'Aurore*

mediately drew the proper conclusions and brought the matter to the attention of his superiors. Thus, the panic-stricken general staff was confronted with a terrible choice: either bring Esterhazy to trial, admit to a gross miscarriage of justice, and then face the disastrous political consequences; or attempt a cover-up in order to save face. After Picquart's disclosure, the general staff applied the most outrageous forms of coercion in an attempt to silence him. These included transferring him to Tunisia, dismissing him from the service, and, finally, threatening his life. But the courageous colonel held firm. Providing an account of the inquiry to his close confidants, who then leaked the news, Picquart fought his battle for truth. Meanwhile, Lucien Herr had finally persuaded Jaurès of Dreyfus's innocence and Blum that the case was politically important. Through numerous articles and intense public activity, Blum and other Parisian intellectuals, including Zola, Clemenceau, and Anatole France, raised the specter of scandal.

Now, the political leadership of the country became nervous. Fearful of implication due to their own negligence, the governmental leaders joined in the cover-up on the side of the army general staff. As France split into two warring camps — the Dreyfusards and anti-Dreyfusards — the public was in an uproar. The military felt pressure to put Esterhazy on trial and also review the Dreyfus conviction. Then, in yet another unfair trial by a military court, Dreyfus's appeal was rejected and Esterhazy was acquitted.

It was then that Émile Zola published his bold article "J'accuse" ("I Accuse") in Clemenceau's newspaper, *L'Aurore*. There, he described the whole sordid affair and revealed the names of those military leaders who had conspired in the cover-up. Indeed, that piece by Émile Zola has become nothing less than a historical monument to the cause of justice.

The affair now entered a new stage. It was no longer a matter of some judicial decision regarding a crime. Instead, it was a question of whether justice for the individual outweighed the certainty of a na-

Deuxième Année. — Numéro 87   **Cinq Centimes**   **JEUDI 13 JANVIER 1898**

Directeur
ERNEST VAUGHAN
ABONNEMENTS

Directeur
ERNEST VAUGHAN
LES ANNONCES SONT REÇUES :
142 — Rue Montmartre — 143
AUX BUREAUX DU JOURNAL

L'AURORE

Littéraire, Artistique, Sociale

J'Accuse...!

LETTRE AU PRÉSIDENT DE LA RÉPUBLIQUE
Par ÉMILE ZOLA

**LETTRE
A M. FÉLIX FAURE**
Président de la République

Monsieur le Président,

Me permettez-vous, dans ma gratitude pour le bienveillant accueil que vous m'avez fait un jour, d'avoir le souci de votre juste gloire et de vous dire que votre étoile, si heureuse jusqu'ici, est menacée de la plus honteuse, de la plus ineffaçable des taches?

[The remainder of Zola's open letter is set in small type across the following newspaper columns.]

---

tional scandal and the disgrace of the army. The stakes had grown.

"J'accuse" had a sensational international impact and could not be ignored. After some initial hesitation, the army responded by placing Zola on trial for libel. As Blum employed his judicial talents to aid Fernand Labori, the famous lawyer for the defense, the trial turned into a circus.

Reporters from all over the world flocked to the proceedings. Demonstrations were organized by right-wing groups like Les Camelots du Roi (The King's Newsboys). Monarchist and anti-Semitic mobs roamed wild. Literary and political figures of the Left were now insultingly called "intellectuals" — a term used to define those individuals seen as radical, uprooted, cosmopolitan, and loyal only to abstract ideas of truth and justice.

Throughout the trial, Zola and the supporters of Dreyfus lived in constant fear of physical violence. But the fact that the prosecution packed the courtroom with anti-Dreyfusard officers and thugs and that the trial was conducted in a blatantly biased

"J'accuse," Émile Zola's world-famous 1898 denouncement of the French military. Soon after, Zola was prosecuted for libel. Blum assisted in his legal defense, but Zola fled to England after the corrupt court found him guilty.

29

Émile Zola, one of the premier figures of French literature. The biased trial and
exile of Zola changed the
Dreyfus Affair from a military cover-up to a question of
the rights of the individual
versus the rights of the state.

fashion provoked a storm of international outrage,
which increased when Zola was found guilty and
fled to safety in England.

The Dreyfus Affair was now no longer a military
concern. The scandal surrounding Zola's conviction
had made it into a directly political issue. Godefroy
Cavaignac, a member of the War Ministry, was
therefore forced to comment. On the floor of Parliament, he tried to prove the Jewish captain's guilt
by reading from a forged document that was originally used to convict Dreyfus. The Dreyfusards were
deeply disappointed. It looked like the end. Jaurès,
however, recognized that Cavaignac's political

speech had unintentionally opened the affair to public scrutiny. Thus, Jaurès openly tore apart the prosecution's entire case in a brilliant series of articles entitled *Les Preuves* (*The Proofs*).

On August 30, 1898, two members of the army general staff who had been engaged in the cover-up resigned their posts. The next day the author of one of the forgeries, a Colonel Henry, committed suicide. The day after that, Esterhazy fled to England. Then, on September 3, Cavaignac resigned and, within the next two months, two other cabinet ministers followed suit. In 1899 Dreyfus was returned from Devil's Island for a retrial, and he ultimately received a pardon. Nevertheless, it was not until 1906 that

Zola, Fernand Labori (his defense counsel), newspaper publisher Georges Clemenceau, and others arriving at Zola's trial. Though Labori's efforts were in vain, Clemenceau's leftist newspaper coverage made a considerable uproar among intellectuals.

he was formally reinstated into the army and the nightmare came to an end.

But the wounds did not heal. The conservative attitudes of the army remained, while anti-Semitism became a real political issue for the first time in French history. An alliance also formed between the army, the Church, and conservative social classes like the aristocracy, the peasantry, and the "petty bourgeoisie," which was composed of small shopkeepers and minor state officials. It was from these groups that important new organizations of the Right, like Action Française, would draw their mass support.

Blum could already see the traces of a fascist ideology emerging during the Dreyfus Affair. He worried over the extreme nationalism. He despised the anti-Semitism and anti-intellectualism. He despaired over the contempt for the rule of law and the disregard for individual rights. He feared the new tactics of intimidation and mob violence. Indeed, he saw the danger that the Right posed to democracy and socialism.

The Dreyfus Affair demonstrated that there were groups within France with traditional economic, social, and political privileges that could be used to subvert justice. These groups hated democracy and the very idea of material equality. Only by defending both would it become possible to hinder their unfair control over state power. Abolishing their privileges would demand a radical socialist transformation of society. The conclusion of the Dreyfus Affair also showed that under the proper circumstances the state could be used to redress certain grievances and that democratic procedures could check the arbitrary use of power.

All of this seemed to show the need for a political commitment. The Dreyfus Affair made clear to Blum that progress toward a more just society could not be taken for granted.

Such reflections surely drew Blum to Jaurès and his particular brand of socialism. The young man admired the way in which Jaurès gave those various insights a coherent theoretical form. In the future, no less than his great teacher, Blum would stand for the integral connection between socialism and democracy.

The close of the Dreyfus Affair had led Jaurès to begin his monumental *Socialist History of the French Revolution*. That made perfect sense, because the affair showed the continuing relevance of the French Revolution and its republican ideals. Still, Jaurès knew that the primary goal of socialism was to forward the general demands of workers. Those demands essentially involved liberty from excess toil, equality in the distribution of wealth, and public control over the way in which products were produced and economic policies were set. From the socialist viewpoint, such demands were the extension of "liberty, equality, and fraternity" from the realm of political democracy into the realm of economic life. Hence, Jaurès came to understand socialism as the attempt to fulfill the most radical democratic demands of the French Revolution. It was this conception of socialism to which Blum would dedicate himself until the end of his life.

> *I am not sure that in my entire life I have experienced a stronger emotional upheaval.*
> —LÉON BLUM
> on the Dreyfus Affair

The storming of the Bastille, commencement of the French Revolution, 1789. This prison, which at one point housed hundreds of political prisoners, still stands in Paris as a monument to the destruction of despotism. Equality, the Revolution's great theme, inspired Blum and others, who turned to socialism as the only system that could carry France toward true democracy.

A sketch of Blum, whose image became familiar throughout France during the early 1900s. After helping to found the French Section of the International Workers' Organization (SFIO) in 1905, Blum became one of the most outspoken political figures in France.

3

Building a Movement

> The free man is he who does
> not fear to get to the end of
> his thought.
> —LÉON BLUM

During the years that followed the Dreyfus Affair, the antidemocratic threat from the Right fostered a desire for unity among socialists. This, however, meant overcoming what had already become a historical tradition of divisiveness on the Left. Consequently, though the need for a unified party was clear, its creation was no easy task.

At the turn of the century French socialism was split into many parties and factions. Some socialists, like Jaurès and Blum, were committed to building a mass movement that would follow the electoral course and develop unity on the basis of broad socialist and democratic principles. Others, like Édouard Vaillant, sought an immediate revolutionary seizure of state power, while the followers of Jean Allemane rejected parliamentary activity in the name of regional and union forms of organization. There were also more cautious types like Paul Brousse, who wished to further the interests of workers by making compromises with other classes and exerting influence through cabinet posts.

The largest and oldest grouping of French socialists was led by a great organizer named Jules Guesde, and by Karl Marx's son-in-law, Paul Lafargue, who once wrote a delightful satirical pamphlet entitled *The Right to be Lazy*. No less than Jaurès, the followers of Guesde and Lafargue wished to organize a socialist movement that would grow through electoral activity.

THE BETTMANN ARCHIVE

Jean Jaurès, the central figure of unified French socialism. The 25-year-old Blum was introduced to Jaurès by Lucien Herr. Blum was later to say that of all the great men he had met, Jaurès had "the most active, most precise, most penetrating intelligence."

French workers in 1900. The success of socialism in France depended on the leftist parties uniting workers toward a common goal. Rallying the workers was difficult and frustrating work for Blum. Beyond that, the various leftist parties themselves had to be united in order to be victorious.

In contrast to Jaurès, Guesde wanted to separate the interests of workers from all "bourgeois" concerns (like the Dreyfus Affair) and emphasize a particularly crude and orthodox form of Marxism. In the view of Guesde, the new socialist party would refuse to engage in coalitions with bourgeois parties, to squabble over cabinet posts, or to deal with issues outside the direct concern of workers. Thus, the party would keep its principles and so prepare for a future socialist revolution.

Clearly, Jaurès, Blum, and Herr had their work cut out for them. Still, all the major participants were committed activists who had often paid a high price for their principles. Each, after his fashion, sought the best for the working class. The socialist leaders realized that, whatever the differences between them, they also had a great deal in common. Thus, with Jean Jaurès standing in the forefront, the bargaining began.

The result was a compromise. The new party would seek to develop a national following through

Capitalists mutilate the laborer into a fragment of a man, degrade him to the level of an appendage of a machine, destroy every remnant of charm in his work and then turn it into a hated toil.
—KARL MARX
19th-century German political philosopher, in his seminal work *Das Kapital*

Karl Marx, German economist and philosopher. His work *The Communist Manifesto*, published in 1848, formed the intellectual basis of European socialism.

electoral activity and union work. It would emphasize the role of the working class, but still remain open to all people of good will. In this vein, the party would hold out the ideal of a revolutionary transformation of French society, but still seek reforms to alleviate injustice and oppression.

For the socialists, class interest would therefore take primacy over opportunism. The party would refuse to join in coalitions with other classes or accept cabinet posts in a bourgeois government. As a democratic organization, it would naturally allow for many points of view. Nevertheless, the socialist organization would retain its sense of purpose and identity by maintaining an explicit commitment to orthodox Marxism.

Unlike the orthodox Marxists, Jaurès, Blum, and their friends never believed that Marxism was a science. Nor did they accept Marx's claims that the collapse of capitalism and the victory of socialism

Friedrich Engels, Marx's closest friend and collaborator. After Marx's death in 1883, Engels edited and completed Marx's unfinished work *Das Kapital (Capital)*.

were somehow historically inevitable. Instead, Jaurès and Blum saw socialism as an ethical enterprise, the realization of which was by no means certain. Nevertheless, they both agreed that an unregulated market and private control over investment caused basic conflicts of economic interest between workers and capitalists.

Like the Marxists, Jaurès and Blum were appalled that capital was concentrated in the hands of the few, and they believed that the future held economic crises. They too believed in the need for various socioeconomic reforms to protect workers and the unemployed. No less than Marx, Jaurès and Blum also saw the need for a party that might democratically prepare for the transformation of French capitalism to socialism.

Whatever the theoretical disagreements, the practical differences between the followers of Jaurès and the orthodox Marxists were few and not of great significance. Some fundamental basis for agreement existed between the major factions. Otherwise, the unification of French socialism under the acknowledged leadership of Jaurès would have been impossible.

The new party came into existence in 1905. An independent entity, it was unofficially linked to the growing national union movement, the CGT (General Confederation of Workers). Its newspaper was titled *L'Humanité (Humanity)*, which had been founded a few years earlier by Jaurès, Blum, and Herr. Proudly, the party took its place within the recently created international organization of social democratic parties. Hence its name: the French Section of the International Workers' Organization (SFIO).

Blum could have become a political force, with the new party as his springboard of influence. But it was precisely at this time that he retired from politics for nearly a decade. Of course, Blum remained connected to party affairs and performed useful political work as a private lawyer. Nevertheless, except for an occasional speech or article in *L'Humanité*, he really only participated in politics from behind the scenes.

Blum returned to the world of culture. There he leisurely worked on his literary projects. For example, he completed a book on the French novelist Stendhal, which was published in 1914. It was a work that helped establish Stendhal's contemporary importance even as it sought to save him from ideological appropriation by intellectuals of the far Right. Thus, Blum's political concerns did not disappear—though they remained in the background.

It is uncertain why he returned to literary pursuits. Perhaps he was simply tired and needed a rest. Perhaps he wanted time for his family. (In 1896 he married Lise Bloch, who gave birth to their only child, Robert, six years later). Perhaps Blum felt that the great battles were over, that the party leadership was in the sure hands of Jaurès, who represented Blum's own thinking.

There is, however, another probable explanation. The fact is that, in spite of his intellectual commitment and activity during the Dreyfus Affair, Blum was still by temperament and lifestyle more an "engaged" man of letters than a truly political man. It would take the murder of his mentor and the seeming collapse of everything for which he had fought to truly complete the transition.

Leading socialists gather in a Paris restaurant. Jaurès (standing at left) was the focus of the various socialist sects. His SFIO allowed for debate and the exchange of ideas, with the goal of overcoming the barriers between socialist groups, thus consolidating their political strength.

I have no superstitious belief in legality, it has already received too many blows; but I always advise workmen to have recourse to legal means, for violence is the sign of temporary weakness.
— JEAN JAURÈS

4

The Great Betrayal

Internationalism, the vision of a world government that would encompass all nation-states, was another one of those cherished socialist ideals that emerged from the Enlightenment and the French Revolution. The great 18th-century German philosopher Immanuel Kant, a major theoretical influence on Jaurès and Blum, was one who had voiced this idea. "Perpetual peace," Kant believed, could only exist under a world order of republics committed to the rule of law.

The French Revolution took up that call. Beginning in 1789, this uprising was directed against the traditions of the Middle Ages and a political order dominated by the aristocracy. In place of the old order came a new economic system called capitalism, along with a new class of capitalists known as the bourgeoisie. Proclaiming a commitment to democratic principles in the name of "the people," the French Revolution attempted to spread "the rights of man" beyond its own national boundaries.

This quickly produced a violent reaction from nations such as Austria and Prussia (an eastern German state), which were ruled by the old aristocratic

> *In proportion as the antagonism between the classes vanishes, the hostility of one nation to another will come to an end.*
> —KARL MARX
> in the *Manifesto of the Communist Party*, 1848

Blum with his lifelong friend, socialist activist Vincent Auriol. After the SFIO had become firmly established, Blum devoted most of his time to his law practice, while maintaining discreet contact with his activist comrades.

41

order. In concert with England, they waged war based on conservative and nationalist principles. Meanwhile, the French government grew more authoritarian as counterrevolution, subversion, sabotage, hoarding of goods, and illegal financial speculation threatened the war effort. Threatened by invasion from without and chaos from within, the French turned to a young general named Napoleon Bonaparte, who would soon become emperor and attempt to create a United States of Europe. Following Napoleon's defeat in 1815, the capitalist class in Europe soon made its peace with the nation-state and surrendered its earlier ideals.

In *The Communist Manifesto* (published in 1848), however, German philosophers and economists Karl Marx and Friedrich Engels tried to give the old dream new meaning by calling upon workers of the world to unite. Essentially, they believed that the nation-state primarily served the interests of the capitalist class. What's more, they felt that nationalism artificially divided workers, fostered militarism, and so produced wars — whose victims would be the workers themselves.

These two founders of "scientific socialism" went on to form the First International in 1864. A loose democratic grouping of anarchists and socialists of various stripes, it sought to further the organization of workers in many lands. It elected Marx as its first president.

The First International, beset by internal disputes and police harassment, collapsed in 1869. But, following the Franco-Prussian War of 1870–71 (a conflict between France and the newly established German nation), the upsurge in European socialist activity led to the formation of the Second International in 1889. It was considered the most treasured product of the socialist movement and orthodox Marxist ideology. Embodying the vision of a future socialist world, the Second International stood for pacifism, democracy, solidarity, and mutual cooperation among member social democratic parties.

It was therefore an incredible shock when all of its member parties (except the Italian) chose to sup-

The mobilization order of August 1914 is read to Germans in the Berlin Tiergarten. Socialists had agreed to noncompliance, even insurrection, in case of mobilization, but when the time came to defend their nations most rallied back to the flag, putting aside socialist principles.

port their respective nations at the outbreak of World War I. In fact, a relatively unknown Russian exile in Switzerland initially thought the news was mere bourgeois propaganda and suffered a near breakdown when he learned the truth. It was then that Vladimir Ilich Lenin, who would later become the leader of the Russian Revolution, first began to plan the construction of a new and very different Third International, which would have such profound implications for Blum and the SFIO.

But that was for the future. The present harbored war. Following the assassination of the Austrian Archduke Franz Ferdinand in 1914, a chain of events was unleashed that drew all the major European nations into conflict. On the one side there initially stood Russia, France, and Great Britain; on the other the Austro-Hungarian Empire, Germany, and the Ottoman Empire (Turkey).

At the time, none of the participants could really visualize what a world war implied. For decades Eu-

French soldiers firing from the trenches during World War I. Blum had argued that even the deeply pacifist Jaurès, who had been assassinated in 1914, would have condoned mobilization in the face of a German invasion. In a fellow SFIO member's words, the party would never "surrender the most socialist country to the least socialist."

We have been completely faithful to our national duty, without renouncing our international duty, or as I would prefer to say, our human duty.

—LÉON BLUM
defending the Socialist
party's support of French
involvement in World War I

ropean nation-states had jockeyed for economic and political superiority. They had built armies and bullied one another over African and Asian colonies, creating one crisis after another, always stopping short of a major confrontation.

Europe had been at peace since 1871. Everyone initially thought the war of 1914 would be short-lived. The leaders of Europe had no idea that, by the time it was over, four empires would be split up, a revolution would strike the imagination of the war-weary masses, and an entire world would be transformed.

Still, if such blindness was true for the bourgeois politicians, the socialists were no better. Neither Jaurès nor his orthodox Marxist opponents foresaw the dimensions of the conflict or the impotence of the Second International. The situation was totally disheartening. Until the last possible moment, the Second International was issuing peace decrees, and its leaders were talking about the possibility of resistance in the event of war.

Jaurès desperately sought to oppose the descent into madness. He proclaimed the need for a strike, calling upon the working masses to fulfill their international obligations, reminding them that their blood would pay the price for national capitalist ambitions. And then he was assassinated while having

dinner in a café, leaving the SFIO without his bold leadership, moral direction, and sense of purpose.

Could Jaurès's pacifism have carried the day had he lived? It is highly unlikely. The forces that produced the war stood beyond his control. Also, socialists everywhere were unprepared for the choice history would present to them. Clearly they had underestimated the ideological power of nationalism and the role of the nation-state. So too, they had overestimated the organizational importance of the Second International and the strength of that mutual trust necessary for socialist solidarity.

Socialists forgot that the Second International lacked any power to back up its decrees with sanctions. They also forgot that the nation-state could easily use force to crush or ban any party it considered treasonous. In addition, the socialist parties of France and Germany were no longer the small, ragtag, and divided bands of the past. They had become mass organizations of millions of members with a real stake in the preservation of those nation-states

French soldiers capturing a hill in 1917. The war was catastrophic beyond the most frightening nightmare — almost 10 million soldiers were killed, including 1.4 million Frenchmen. When the soldiers returned home disillusioned with a war that appeared pointless, the socialists, who had joined the government in facing the emergency on August 2, 1914, found their prestige severely damaged.

that granted them their reforms and provided them with the possibilities of power. Consequently, setting ideology aside, the real practical interest of these social democratic parties lay with their respective nation-states rather than with the Second International.

There was also the matter of trust. Questions quickly arose over what would happen if the working class of one nation chose pacifism, and another chose war. Forgetting that France was aligned with an ultrareactionary Russian tsar, Guesde looked at Germany and piously proclaimed that the SFIO would never "surrender the most socialist country to the least socialist." Meanwhile, German socialists raised fears of domination by the barbarous Russian tsar, even as they conveniently ignored the imperialist designs of their own leader, Kaiser Wilhelm II, and their nation's alliance with a decrepit Austrian monarchy.

In every major state with a large socialist movement, a truce between the classes was therefore arranged for the duration of the war. In Germany it was called a *Burgfrieden*, in France a *union sacrée*. As in Germany, so in France: Guesde, Vaillant, Brousse, and the rest were overcome with patriotic fever. The values that had sustained the Second International for 25 years suddenly vanished. Everywhere, Marxists and socialists rushed to support their respective governments.

What of Léon Blum? The death of Jaurès on July 31, 1914, two days before France's mobilization decrees, was a devastating blow that brought Blum out of his self-imposed retirement. Unfortunately, however, Blum's conduct during the war years certainly did not constitute the moral highlight of his distinguished career. While Lenin literally stood alone in calling upon the world proletariat to turn the conflict between states into an international class war, a tiny minority — including such socialist luminaries as Rosa Luxemburg, Karl Liebknecht, and Leon Trotsky — faced prison and exile for their commitment to a proletarian pacifism.

As for Blum, he acted no differently than the majority of his socialist comrades. But that was not

the worst of it. There was something uncommonly hypocritical in Blum's attempt to justify himself by claiming that Jaurès would have acted similarly.

Blum apparently believed he had made the correct moral decision. Yet, surveying the terrain, he must also have considered his own political position carefully. After all, Lenin headed what was then merely a small sect, and the majority of pacifist rebels were not in positions of real power.

It must have seemed different for Blum. He was surely aware that the death of Jaurès had created a power vacuum within the SFIO and that he was a contender for his old friend's mantle. Virtually every major leader of the SFIO had endorsed France's role in the conflict. For right or wrong, Blum must have recognized the potentially disas-

While most leftist leaders rallied to their country's defense, Vladimir Ilich Lenin, the Russian communist leader, stood alone in calling for defiance to the war. Afterwards, he gained in reputation as one of the few leftist leaders who had stuck to the original antiwar principles of the left-wing parties.

Lenin (seated center) and members of his communist underground in 1895, part of the movement that would seize power in the Russian Revolution of 1917. Lenin believed that the only way for leftist doctrine to succeed was to destroy the existing oppressive government. The more moderate Blum felt that European governments should not be destroyed but used to gain power, an important break with Leninism.

trous consequences of breaking with the party majority and, by implication, with its working-class constituency. Thus, Blum once more became a political man.

In accordance with the spirit of the union sacrée, the SFIO joined the government of "national defense," which was led by Clemenceau. In return, the party received certain cabinet posts. Essentially in combination with his colleague Marcel Sembat, Blum ran the Ministry of Public Works and used that position to good advantage.

Blum was now forcibly introduced to economics and the thinking of industrialists. More than that, however, Blum learned about the inner workings of governmental institutions. Timidly, he sought progressive — if not socialist — administrative reforms

along with a degree of state control over capitalist enterprise and profit sharing for workers. Blum employed his new position to expand his influence and contacts within the SFIO. Indeed, within a few years after the war, Blum would become the acknowledged successor to Jaurès.

But the party could not contain the forces its own choices had helped to unleash. As the war dragged on, the working masses became disillusioned. The initial thrill of battle dulled before rising economic costs and longer death lists. Grumbling could be heard everywhere as the agitation of pacifists and revolutionary exiles began to take effect. Strikes occurred with increasing regularity, as did rebellion in the ranks of the armed forces.

Elements within European social democracy began to recognize the sounds of dissent and responded to their leadership with varying degrees of militancy. Though a disgust with the war was rapidly rising, however, it was still unclear how much support the rebels actually enjoyed. The bulk of those party officials who initially supported the war effort were now trapped by their previous political decisions and the self-justifying propaganda they had used.

Blum tended to maintain allegiance to his original position. Even had he changed his mind, it probably would not have made a significant difference for the SFIO's immediate future. It was already too late when the thunderbolt struck.

He was there, nervous, feverish. His eyes shone with a prodigious gleam, a Dantesque flame, his face was pale, the muscles tense without moving; his mustache revealed a sensual mouth which seemed to be savoring the taste of a voluptuous prey. This living statue of political passion, this symbolic figure, deeply animated and agitated within, was perhaps terrifying but had in it a kind of concentrated splendor.

—HUBERT BOURGIN
French socialist, describing in his memoirs Blum's appearance as a member of the public works ministry

5

A New Direction

The thunderbolt was the Russian Revolution of 1917. The surrender of Germany and her allies in 1918 was really an anticlimax for the socialist movement. Indeed, speaking practically, the difference between victory and defeat meant little to the decimated working masses of Europe.

France had suffered nearly 5 million casualties during the war, and the entire continent stood close to economic collapse. In the wake of such devastation, the old parties and their values appeared bankrupt.

Years of war for what? Where were the jobs for the returning soldiers? The workers were even worse off than before. Often forgetting their own joy at the war's outbreak, they now resented the timidity and hypocrisy of their old leaders. What had happened to the principles of the once proud and vibrant socialist movement?

The workers of Europe turned to the east. While their own social democratic leaders were collaborating with the bourgeoisie, Lenin and Trotsky had never wavered in their internationalist commitments. In backward Russia, their audacious Bol-

> *A Socialist can feel in himself the greatest love for the Russian Revolution, be resolved to protect it by all means, without agreeing that Russian revolutionary methods are applicable to socialism.*
> —LÉON BLUM
> quoted from an editorial in
> *L'Humanité*, October 1920

Blum was one of the few Frenchmen who opposed the Treaty of Versailles, which imposed impossible penalties on Germany. He remembered the rise of the Right in his own country after the humiliating Franco-Prussian war settlement and correctly predicted the same reaction to the Versailles Treaty in Germany.

A victory celebration in Paris. After enduring 47 years of shame from their defeat by the Germans during the Franco-Prussian War, the French were primed to take revenge on their neighboring enemy. Fraternity and equality, some of the basic tenets of socialism, were nowhere to be found when the French convinced the Allies to impose a harsh treaty on Germany.

shevik party had even succeeded in creating a new, dynamic revolutionary "dictatorship of the proletariat and peasantry." At last, a worker's state! At last, a ray of hope amid universal destruction and despair!

The mood among workers had become more radical. The survival of the SFIO demanded that it respond to the new political climate. This implied a change in political direction, which Blum would articulate in speeches and writings like *To Be A Socialist* (published in 1919).

Under Blum's leadership that new direction would seek to break the connection between the SFIO and its former bourgeois allies in the union sacrée. In 1919 the French left was divided into two main parties, Blum's SFIO, which was also known as the Socialist party, and the Radical, or Socialist Radical, party. Despite its name, the Radical party was not devoted to hard-line socialism, and Blum believed that the Radicals had a bourgeois ideology. The SFIO would have to forward its own unique identity, which clearly demanded the articulation of a new and more radical program of social and economic reform. In addition, in opposition to those who wished to form a separate French communist movement, this new direction would emphasize the need to maintain the unity of the working class along with the link between socialism and democracy. Interestingly enough, in combination, these very ideas would ultimately serve as a foundation for the SFIO's "popular front" policy of the future.

In a certain way, the first points were the easiest to achieve. The differences between the SFIO and its former allies soon became quite clear-cut. Indeed, this was the case from the standpoint of both domestic and foreign policy.

Following World War I, the Right surrendered its commitment to reinstate the monarchy. Still, its supporters continued to attack the Third Republic along with all attempts to achieve much-needed democratic and economic reforms. Ignoring the costs of World War I, the conservatives of France gloried in victory and dreamed of conquest. Thus, in terms of foreign policy, the Right — along with many liberals in the Radical party — immediately gave their support to the proposed Treaty of Versailles.

That treaty tried to fix blame for starting the war on Germany and prevent that country from ever again forming an army. It also sought enormous monetary reparations, which Germany could never possibly pay, to compensate the victorious nations for their economic losses. Finally, the treaty demanded that Germany surrender all its colonies and certain domestic territories — including the disputed region of Alsace-Lorraine, which France had lost following the Franco-Prussian War.

Blum never tried either to deny or retract the positions that he and the SFIO had taken with regard to World War I. But, in opposing the Treaty of Versailles, Blum and the SFIO made a clear break with the nationalists. He argued that the SFIO had entered the union sacrée not out of a desire for con-

The Big Four (left to right): Prime Minister David Lloyd George of Britain, Prime Minister Vittorio Orlando of Italy, French Premier Georges Clemenceau, and United States President Woodrow Wilson. The Allied leaders gathered in Paris to negotiate the treaty that would end World War I.

quest or territories, but rather in order to defend France. He knew that economic greed and political ambition among all participants had contributed to creating the conflict.

It was also obvious to him that this harsh treaty would not further the cause of future peace. Instead, it would only humiliate and impoverish Germany. Indeed, Blum realized that the treaty would only help the German Right by creating a climate of revenge similar to what he had experienced in his own country during the Dreyfus Affair. Consequently, in taking this stand, Blum not only tried to reaffirm his party's commitment to simple justice and internationalist principles, but proved something of a prophet as well.

Shaping the SFIO's unique identity, however, also involved political decisions on the domestic front. Though he personally felt that the party should be more flexible, Blum and the SFIO decided to refuse any postwar collaboration with the liberal Radical party. Thus, even though the French electoral system tended to provide incentives for such coalitions, the SFIO decided not to engage in "ministerial politics" — whereby various cabinet posts are exchanged for a party's support of a ruling governmental coalition.

Opportunist elements within the party correctly claimed that such a stance would condemn the SFIO to defeat in the next elections. But Blum looked beyond the immediate present. He wished to preserve the party's radical identity for the future.

In the 1919 parliamentary elections, however, a coalition of rightist and centrist groups gained control of the Chamber of Deputies. (The French Parliament was composed of two bodies, the Chamber of Deputies and the Senate. The former body tended to hold greater power.) Although the SFIO's representation in the national government declined, Blum won a seat in the Chamber of Deputies for the first time. He also became leader of the SFIO.

The SFIO's shift toward a more radical image affected its economic program. Blum therefore sought increased national control over the economy, a tax on capital, and various other legislation to benefit

Léon Blum stood out by virtue of his knowledge, his cultivation, and, above all, his intellectual honesty.

— JEAN LONGUET
French socialist, on why Blum, a relative newcomer to the SFIO, had become its leader in 1919

workers. They were shrewd demands, since he knew that his former capitalist allies would reject such policy proposals as too costly. Thus, while separating his party from its former allies, Blum tried to give the SFIO a more radically socialist posture to offset criticism from the communists and maintain the unity of the party.

That, however, proved nothing more than a dream. In the years immediately following World War I it became apparent that the old party leadership had clearly lost control of the membership. Disgusted by the SFIO's war policy and inspired by the Soviet example, revolutionary sentiments grew more powerful. Sympathy for the bold Bolsheviks increased even more when the previously warring Western capitalist nations agreed to mount an anti-

Jubilant French troops occupy the Ruhr, Germany's industrial center, after the signing of the Treaty of Versailles.

Soviet crusade against the new state. This intensified what had already become a ferocious civil war
between the counterrevolutionary Whites and the
communist Reds that threatened to destroy the new
workers' state. Indeed, that threat seemed to justify
the frankly authoritarian and antidemocratic policies of the new regime.

"Comrade Lenin cleans the world of squalor." Through-out the 1920s communist propaganda attempted to am-plify the division of the classes to create resentment against capitalist and impe-rialist governments, here being swept away by Lenin.

The workers had already lost their faith in the SFIO. Initially, the workers scoffed at the changes that Blum wished to fashion. Indeed, his program must have appeared incredibly self-serving. Distancing the SFIO from its former allies made the party seem like a rat jumping the sinking ship. Calling for more radical reforms looked like just another unprincipled move to outflank the young communist movement. Affirming the traditional link between socialism and democracy appeared as merely another trick to condemn real revolutionaries and justify the old politicians of the union sacrée. As for the appeal to unity, it was the only possible stance for a party that was losing its membership to a new one. Thus, the SFIO's change of direction came too late for most workers.

Though Blum opposed the anti-Soviet crusade and tried to better the ties between the Soviet Union and the capitalist world, things only grew worse for the SFIO in 1919. Support for the embattled Soviet Union seemed the logical course for every radical socialist and worker. Inflamed with dreams of an emancipated communist future, repulsed by recent memories of the social democratic past, workers revolted in almost every nation in Europe. In that same year, workers around the world were thrilled when Lenin formed the Third International, which called for the formation of national communist parties.

A bitter split took place in 1920 at the SFIO party convention in Tours. The dissidents constituted the majority. Among them were many of the finest and most militant activists of the SFIO. The group left to form the French Communist party (PCF). They took with them almost all the older party's funds as well as *L'Humanité*, which became — and still remains—the official newspaper of the PCF.

Though the SFIO received support from aligned unions, its losses in the general election of 1921 were substantial. The party of Jaurès seemed on the verge of extinction. Truly, the SFIO was paying a high price for its part in the "great betrayal."

Let us know how to abstain from words that wound and lacerate, actions that injure, everything that would be a fratricidal division. In spite of all, let us remain brothers, brothers separated by a quarrel which is cruel but which is a family quarrel, and whom a common hearth someday will reunite.
—LÉON BLUM
pleading for SFIO party unity at the Tours congress, December 1920

6

Between Communism and Fascism

American writers like Ernest Hemingway and Gertrude Stein wrote that World War I created a "lost generation." Bewildered, unemployed, cynical about the values and movements of the past, the returning soldiers looked for something new in which they could place their faith.

Some felt that the entire experience of the war was nothing more than a terrible waste. Their lives were shattered, but they still retained a sense of class solidarity. They despised the capitalist system and those who had made enormous profits from the war. Seething with revolutionary impatience, they swore that the next time they fought, if ever, it would only be to destroy the source of such catastrophes. Some of these people entered the new communist movement, perhaps returned to the social democrats later, and generally remained on the left.

There were others, however, who saw the matter differently. They hated both socialism and capitalism, which to them seemed to threaten time-honored national traditions. They hated democracy and republican institutions. They listened when propagandists of the Right told them that Jews con-

> *Morality may consist solely in the courage of making a choice.*
> —LÉON BLUM

As Blum rose to power, he saw the role of socialism as unifying society, distributing the wealth more equally rather than inciting the working class to destroy the rich. He was opposed on the Left by communists who held that nothing short of revolution would lead to equality.

trolled the banks and also dominated the Left. The disgruntled soldiers thought of the Rothschild family of bankers, then they thought of Léon Blum, and that was proof enough.

These men of the Right, however, also felt that the war had somehow justified their lives, that the "brotherhood of the trenches" had brought out their best qualities of discipline, combat, heroism, and nationalism. Indeed, they felt that the experience of this brotherhood separated them forever from civilian existence and the decadent world of bourgeois "Jewish" comfort and democratic complacency.

It is true that the traditional liberal and conservative parties did not simply disappear. But until the establishment of the Popular Front the SFIO remained caught between the communists on the extreme left and the fascists on the extreme right. Thus, against a rising tide of authoritarian thinking, Blum became the spokesperson for a socialist vision that was bound to democratic republican principles.

At the beginning of the 1920s, the SFIO's main concern was the communists. Blum shared neither temperamental similarities nor theoretical inclination with Lenin and his Bolshevik followers. Indeed, Lenin's thinking had developed in a very different context than his own.

Marx and his orthodox followers basically took it for granted that the socialist revolution would take place in an advanced capitalist country, where the working class was in the majority. This was what justified the socialist revolution since, in contrast to all others, it would be the work of the people rather than a tiny minority or some political clique. The socialist commitment to democracy was therefore a matter of principle. Always accountable to its working-class constituency, the socialist, democratic party that Marx envisioned would never be afraid to air its internal differences in public. As for the workers, schooled in electoral politics, they would build their power gradually. Then, after their party had finally assumed control of society's political institutions, they would carry out the revolution swiftly, with as little bloodshed as possible. The so-

Our mission is to throw ourselves with persistence and diligence into the tasks in Parliament, to defend the rights and interests of the working class which are constantly threatened or under attack, to bar the way to all enterprises directed against it, to spare no effort to transform into positive legislation even the smallest token of justice and progress.
—LÉON BLUM
describing the goals of the SFIO in February 1923

Soldiers of a German revolutionary faction guard the Imperial Palace in Berlin, 1919. Europe was in chaos after the war, with economies in tatters, unemployment climbing, and people disillusioned with their governments. Historically, such a situation has bred revolution—or dictatorship.

cial democratic party might have to use the new state, which it controlled, against capitalist counterrevolutionaries, but never against the working class itself. Indeed, for orthodox Marxists, the new "dictatorship of the proletariat" was justified only insofar as it extended the democratic control of workers over society and its production process.

Prewar Russia, however, was the most economically backward of all the major nation-states. It was populated by a huge peasantry, a small though dynamic working class, a weak bourgeoisie, and a worthless aristocracy. Lacking even the most elementary democratic traditions, imperial Russia was ruled by a tsar and his ruthless secret police.

Conditions were therefore very different than in western Europe, and the possibilities for building a mass social democratic party that would school the working class in democratic traditions simply did not exist. Thus, as early as 1902, Lenin had come to the conclusion that revolutionary change in Russia demanded a "party of a new type." Given the repressive circumstances, the party member would have to exhibit a special type of commitment. He would act as a "professional revolutionary intellectual," who would keep the goal of revolution before the eyes of the masses. In this sense, Lenin's followers viewed themselves as members of a vanguard party.

This vanguard would organize itself in numerous small groups, or cells, to escape detection by the secret police. The party was structured so that sug-

> *The history of all countries shows that the working class, exclusively by its own effort, is able to develop only trade union consciousness, i.e., the conviction that it is necessary to combine in unions, fight the employers, and strike to compel the government to pass necessary labor legislation.*
> —V. I. LENIN
> Bolshevik leader, in his 1902 treatise *What Is To Be Done?*

Éditions du Parti Socialiste (S. F. I. O.)

LÉON BLUM

—❖—

INDEXED IN VF

Bolchevisme

et

Socialisme

(5ᵉ ÉDITION)

PARIS
—
LIBRAIRIE POPULAIRE DU PARTI SOCIALISTE
12, Rue Feydeau, (2ᵉ)
—
1931

Prix : 0 fr. 50

**"Bolshevism and Social-
ism," a pamphlet written by
Blum explaining the position
of his party. Blum was care-
ful to define the distinctions
between his goal of modify-
ing the government and the
communist doctrine of pre-
paring for the moment when
the government could be
toppled.**

gestions would flow from those cells up to the central committee, which would then make all final policy decisions. Lenin also believed that debate and criticism should take place within the cells. Under what was called democratic centralism, however, all members were ultimately pledged to support the leadership's decisions in public.

The party was thus run from the top down. But, as far as Lenin was concerned, conditions in Russia at that time dictated this form of organization. He also genuinely believed that his vanguard party would necessarily embody the true revolutionary interests of workers. He assumed that the vanguard would preserve the revolutionary goal by shielding party members from the temptation to emphasize simply economic reforms and union activity.

Ironically it was Trotsky, an enemy of Lenin at the time, who saw the real implications of his future leader's organizational theory. The party would become a substitute for the working class, the central committee would become a substitute for the party, and finally a dictator would become the substitute for the central committee. That was the price for excluding the mass of workers from democratic participation in the party.

Still, under Lenin, discipline was maintained by trust. The party membership would trust in the revolutionary commitment of the central committee. The leadership would trust in the unquestioning loyalty of the base. Indeed, as far as the radical European working class was concerned, there were good reasons to trust the Bolsheviks.

Lenin and his comrades had spent years in jail and exile. They had adamantly opposed World War I. They had carried through a revolution. All this served to confirm Lenin's convictions among those who felt betrayed by social democracy. Therefore, the dissidents within the SFIO looked to Lenin and the Bolsheviks with admiration.

They felt that the interests of the international working class were fundamentally linked to those of the new Soviet state and its "temporary" dictatorship. Remembering the consequences that had derived from the powerlessness of the Second International, they recognized the need for discipline and obedience to an organization that stood beyond narrow, national interests. Consequently, from the time of its founding, the French Communist party proudly considered itself an organization that would serve the Third International and Soviet policy interests.

The desire to gain support for his imperiled regime and the growth of revolutionary activity abroad were the principal reasons why Lenin decided to form his Communist International. In doing so, however, he tried to apply the same organizational formula that had worked in Russia to all socio-economic conditions. Thus, in the same way that his original Russian cells had obeyed the instructions of the central committee, so too would other national communist parties comply with the decisions of the Third International.

It was against this grand conception, with its initial successes, that Blum attempted to maintain the unity of the SFIO, along with the connection between socialism and democracy. This was the theme of perhaps his most brilliant speech, which was given at the stormy SFIO convention of 1920 at Tours. The speech could not prevent the rupture from taking place. In fact, it only widened the division between socialists and communists, one that has carried over into the present.

At Tours, Blum claimed that socialism could not exist without a mass working-class party committed to democracy. Amid jeers and howls, he questioned the type of obedience demanded by Lenin's Third International and maintained that the new Soviet dictatorship was anything but temporary in character. Then, in a phrase that would make him fa-

THE BETTMANN ARCHIVE

Lenin's tomb in Red Square. Lenin was the undisputed leader of world communism. With his death in 1924 came a battle among factions in the Soviet Union, each attempting to destroy the others to solidify its own position.

Joseph Stalin, leader of the Soviet Union after the death of Lenin. On his deathbed, Lenin had warned that his old protege's lust for power was dangerous. Despite the warning, no faction was strong enough to oppose Stalin's bloody rise to power.

mous, Blum said that he and his followers would keep the "old house" in order until the time when the rebels would choose to return.

Calling forth the images of Jaurès and Guesde, he insisted that socialism express the will of the people and educate the masses in the school of public life. That, however, the socialist leader considered impossible without democratic decision making, the existence of multiple parties, and civil liberties. Indeed, according to him, the party was the servant of the working class — not the other way around.

But Blum also noted something else. It is a point of great significance, usually forgotten, that helps explain the bitter relations between communists and social democrats. Indeed, he emphasized that the difference between the two movements lay not only in the respective ideas, but in their styles.

Because they considered themselves the embodiment of the true interests of the working class, the Bolsheviks chose to consider all parties in Europe that did not conform to their ideology as counterrevolutionary. Anything therefore was considered permissible in the struggle against the party's enemies, including lies, slander, and betrayals. Thus, beginning with Lenin, a vicious style developed — one that Blum could not tolerate and one that he believed would ultimately corrupt the working class.

The Bolshevik hard-line style only became more extreme after the 1917 Revolution. It was then, with the creation of national communist parties under the umbrella of the Third International, that the Bolsheviks found themselves in competition with the European social democratic movement. As far as Blum was concerned, the propaganda campaign aimed against him and his followers — which would continue off and on until his death — broke all the rules of socialist solidarity and common decency. Indeed, this communist campaign seemed to complement perfectly the disgusting propaganda assaults that he endured from the Right.

The communist style, however, soon had internal repercussions as well. Changing times demanded changed tactics or a new ideological line. Since the

Judges at a purge trial, a frequent occurrence in the Soviet Union during the administration of Stalin. To consolidate his strength, Stalin purged the party repeatedly, dragging anyone who represented the least opposition to him before sham trials that invariably ended with a death sentence and the firing squad.

Soviet party and the Third International were structured in an authoritarian fashion, it was easy to implement such changes. Unfortunately, as the demand for party conformity grew following Lenin's death in 1924, each such change meant the instant condemnation of those who had supported the earlier policy.

What was true inside the Soviet Union became true for the member parties of the Third International as well. Since the Communist International was basically controlled from Moscow, each shift in the Soviet line meant a purge of every national communist movement. Members then either had to confess publicly their previous deviations or face expulsion — and sometimes both. This became routine, and the penalties even more severe, once Joseph Stalin, Lenin's successor as head of the Soviet Union, took full charge of the Communist International in 1928.

From 1921 to 1928, the European member parties of the Communist International, or Comintern as it came to be called, gave loyal support to the Soviet Union and the struggle against imperialism. Despite its revolutionary propaganda, the Comintern emphasized union activity and the creation of mass parties. Unfortunately, however, that propaganda began to sound hollow as times improved during the mid-1920s. Also, as internal purges sapped the strength of the communist movement, the PCF began to appear as little more than an authoritarian version of the SFIO. The PCF began to lose votes and squander the momentum with which it started in 1920. A change seemed necessary.

> *For the first time in all socialist history, you conceive of terror not as a measure of last resort only but as a means of government.*
> —LÉON BLUM
> on the Bolshevik party's dictatorial rule of the Soviet Union

7

Prelude to Unity

The words that Blum spoke at Tours were becoming true. Workers began returning to the "old house." In the elections of 1924, his policies produced results. The SFIO nearly doubled its representation in the Chamber of Deputies, and reaffirmed its status against the PCF. Nevertheless, the elections made it clear that conservative coalitions would still dominate France.

Committed to opposing "ministerial politics," the SFIO's victory strengthened the division between the reformist and militant factions within it. The former wished to enter coalitions, receive cabinet posts, build the SFIO's parliamentary influence, and perhaps achieve more reforms. The latter wanted to remain in opposition to all coalitions and emphasize the need for a revolutionary seizure of power. Clearly, the SFIO needed a coherent strategy that would affirm its sense of purpose.

It was in 1926, at the SFIO congress at Bellevilloise, that Blum drew what would become a famous distinction between the "exercise of power" and "conquest of power." Blum stated that the SFIO should pursue its own goals within Parliament but

UPI/BETTMANN NEWSPHOTOS

Italy's Benito Mussolini, Europe's first fascist dictator, addresses a crowd in Rome. Mussolini had seized power in 1922 by leading a fascist march on the capital city. His administration appeared to bring prosperity to Italy, and many in France openly admired his example.

Buoyed by the encouraging results of the 1924 elections, Blum redoubled his efforts to bring his party into the forefront of French politics. His task was hampered by factionalism in the SFIO and by Soviet leader Joseph Stalin's attempts to divide Europe's leftist movement.

should not become involved in coalitions led by other parties. While so involved in the parliamentary process, the party would continue to build the political consciousness of the workers and to secure the most basic reforms necessary for the transition to a new order. Only then could the revolutionary conquest (or assumption) of power take place, based on the mass support of the majority of French men and women.

His concern with the conquest of power and his refusal to take part in cabinets in a government dominated by capitalist parties separated Blum from the less radical reformists within his party. At

UPI/BETTMANN NEWSPHOTOS

Hunger marchers in Paris. While capitalists were attempting to salvage their own fortunes, most of France's laborers had no jobs and no money. The angry, unemployed masses gave strength to the socialist movement, which stood for reforms that would force the government to address the needs and demands of the common worker.

the same time, his emphasis on assuming governmental responsibilities and exercising power through legal parliamentary channels distinguished him from the SFIO radical militants. Indeed, this stance came to define the center position of the SFIO.

Blum maintained that the exercise of power could only occur with the SFIO at the head of a coalition, since the attempt to create socialism would be challenged by capitalist forces. Still, the implications of Blum's approach gave his party a certain political flexibility. This became evident during the election of 1926, the year in which Lucien Herr died.

The situation was serious. The reformist wing of the SFIO was correct in stating that stemming a powerful conservative tide meant supporting the Radicals, who alone could form a government. The militant wing, however, was also correct in claiming that taking cabinet posts in a Radical government would endanger the identity that Blum had tried to cultivate for the SFIO.

Blum found a solution. He called upon the SFIO to support the liberal Radical party in a "coalition of one minute" — the time it takes to cast a vote. What came to be known as the "cartel of the Left" therefore produced a government dominated by Radicals, in which the SFIO held no cabinet posts. Maintaining that "support is not participation," Blum defined a new approach for the SFIO. Indeed, workers seemed to admire Blum's mixture of practical opposition to conservatism and emphasis on socialist principles.

The PCF was left out in the cold. The communists complained about the timidity of the SFIO and urged them to act in a more forcefully radical way. Still, the PCF did not really offer much of an alternative solution.

This had become obvious by 1928, the year in which Stalin really took charge of the communist movement in Europe. The fact that European revolutions had failed seemed to justify the new leader's concern with building "socialism in one country." That, however, left the PCF with no real independent political role to play. Indeed, as Blum predicted

AP/WIDE WORLD

Adolf Hitler, leader of the fascist Nazi party in Germany. Like Mussolini, Hitler was admired by many who saw salvation in a totalitarian government. The brutality fostered by Hitler's regime was seen as a fair price to pay for prosperity, so long as it was directed at others.

69

in 1920, the PCF was now totally dependent upon Moscow for its policies.

This was a particularly serious matter given Stalin's plans for the Soviet Union. Despite new propaganda that suggested that capitalism had "stabilized," he saw his country encircled by enemies. Talking peace, he feared war. Thus, Stalin ultimately decided to industrialize the still underdeveloped Soviet Union by whatever means were necessary.

That domestic policy, however, had implications for Soviet foreign affairs. Essentially, Stalin wanted to buy time. This meant trying to play off one capitalist nation against another. Indeed, that policy led to a decision that would profoundly affect the struggle against fascism for the next eight years.

In 1928 the Comintern charged Europe's social democratic parties with being "twin brothers" with the fascists. From this perspective, the European communists would no longer appear as mere authoritarian versions of the social democrats. Comintern propaganda would now make the difference between these two movements of the working class

More and more, looking at the world, one has the impression of an audience which is somewhat bored, somewhat disappointed, somewhat impatient, waiting restlessly for the end of one act and at the same time listening to the stagehands behind the scenes arranging the scenes for the act that is to follow.

—LÉON BLUM
speaking in
December 1932

"Clochards," or tramps, inhabit the streets of Paris during the 1930s. Economies all over the world were rocked by the depression that had struck in 1929. The inability of France's industrial base to meet the crisis caused workers to rise against the democratic order, with some even calling for fascism.

du travail du pain!

/OTEZ POUR LE SOCIALISTE S.F.I.(

LE CANDIDAT :

"Work and Bread" — a 1932 campaign poster for Blum's SFIO. Depicting a prisoner behind barbed wire, this poster denounces the totalitarian policies of Stalinist communism, while promising the two most desired things in postwar France — a paying job and food.

shockingly clear: The communists would stand for revolution and freedom; the social democrats would stand for fascism.

Of course, Stalin conveniently forgot that the socialists supported democracy, while the fascists opposed republics. According to Stalinist logic, however, that type of difference was irrelevant. What really mattered was that both movements were critical of the Soviet Union.

This new line meant that the communists should now treat both the social democratic and the fascist movements as mortal enemies. The communists would therefore refuse to engage in any joint activity with the social democrats, whom they considered fascists (or "social fascists"). The consequences of this change in Soviet tactics were terrible, especially following the beginning of a worldwide depression in 1929.

This was particularly the case in Germany, where the effects of the depression hit earlier than in France. The German republic witnessed losses by the liberal and more moderately conservative parties to the surging Nazis — the fascist National Socialist German Workers' Party, led by Adolf Hitler — while the social democrats lost votes to the communists. In 1932 the Nazis emerged as the largest party. A coalition of social democrats and communists, with perhaps some support from the liberals, might have kept the Nazis from power. Unfortunately, however, Moscow's decision to maintain the "social fascist" line made such a coalition impossible and led directly to Hitler's triumph.

What did Stalin gain from this policy? Hitler's victory would cause confusion and friction among the nations of Europe. They would become preoccupied with Germany, allowing Stalin to buy some time for the Soviet Union to industrialize. Indeed,

French fascists on parade in 1934. France has always had a strong element of authoritarianism, and rightist groups like Action Française appealed to this strain. Spouting anti-Semitic and antileftist explanations for the nation's troubles, these groups gained a considerable following.

SNARK/ART RESOURCE

Hitler's triumph also served to increase Stalin's bargaining power in terms of any future alliances.

As usual, however, Stalin refused to give the real reasons for his decision. Instead, he justified his policy in revolutionary terms. He told his membership that Hitler's regime could not possibly last more than five years, and then "After Hitler, Us!" Except for those dissidents who were quickly purged, the communist membership believed Stalin. Indeed, the German communists obediently accepted a suicidal policy that led to the appointment of Hitler as chancellor in 1933.

It seemed that France was next. As 1933 turned into 1934, and 1934 into 1935, German exiles flocked to Paris. They were Jews, antifascist activists of various political persuasions, writers, and intellectuals. They fostered the conviction that Hitler had crushed internal opposition and that the regime would surely last more than five years. Through cultural and political activity, they tried to create a climate of resistance and solidarity.

Soon, a combination of frustration and fear gripped the French working class. People started to realize the great mistake Stalin had made. At the same time, the Soviet leader was becoming worried by Hitler's increasingly vicious anti-Bolshevik propaganda and with his decision to rearm Germany despite the terms laid down in the Treaty of Versailles.

All those sentiments came to a head on February 6, 1934, following the public disclosure of the sensational Stavisky scandal on the left, with its rumors of financial speculation and fraud. It was on this day that the rightest Action Française staged huge demonstrations and a violent march on the Chamber of Deputies and called for an end to the "corrupt republic." Severe clashes left 14 dead and 1,300 injured. The storming of the Chamber had nearly succeeded, and there is little doubt that if it had, the final result would have been an authoritarian government or a fascist dictatorship supported by the army.

Fear struck the Left. Hurriedly, a counterdemonstration was organized on February 9, and another

THE BETTMANN ARCHIVE

The German novelist Heinrich Mann was one of the many intellectuals who attacked the rise of fascism in Europe. A demonstration in Paris on July 14, 1935, drew hundreds of thousands of marchers proclaiming the cause of leftist unity. This event led to the formation of the Popular Front coalition.

A demonstration celebrating the victory of the Popular Front. Riding a crest of popularity, Blum now faced the task of carrying out an economic policy that would appeal to the masses, appease the dangerous Right, and not crack the fragile leftist coalition by alienating communist support.

on February 12, in which communists were instructed to participate along with social democrats. Tactfully, the PCF leadership tried to soften Moscow's line. Meanwhile, though justifiably suspicious of the communists, Blum came forth as a strong proponent of joint action between the two working-class parties.

As those Soviet party bureaucrats who had originally proposed the "social fascist" thesis feared for their positions and lives, the call for unity arose from almost every quarter. In 1935 an antifascist international conference was organized. The German novelist Heinrich Mann, brother of the Nobel Prize-winner Thomas Mann, stood in the forefront. André Gide, now firmly identified with the Left, and Henri Barbusse were among those who took part in a demonstration of unity on July 14, 1935. Indeed, this was an enormous event that included speeches by many of the most famous writers in the Western world.

The groundwork for a new policy had therefore already been laid before the Seventh Congress of the Comintern met in August 1935. After the visit to Moscow of French Premier Pierre Laval, Stalin dropped his stubborn opposition to a larger French defense budget and allowed the PCF to join in forming a leftist coalition called the National Committee for Popular Unity, which would become known as the Popular Front. It was really only then that the Soviet leader explicitly recognized the threat from the Right.

Stalin, however, was never one to directly admit a mistake. Support for the Popular Front was one thing, direct alliance with the SFIO another. The PCF was therefore prohibited from either accepting any cabinet posts or participating in the new government. Still, the Seventh Congress of the Communist International formally ratified what had occurred on July 14, 1935, when communists, socialists, and liberals came together to commemorate the French Revolution with a declaration to act as a "popular front against fascism."

Braving a hot summer sun, Blum listens to a speaker at a Popular Front peace demonstration. By the mid-1930s, militant nationalism throughout Europe was propelling the continent closer to a second world war.

8

The Popular Front

The Right was horrified, the workers ecstatic, over the May 1936 elections. The combination of conservative and fascist parties won 222 seats in the Chamber of Deputies. The Popular Front coalition received 386, with the SFIO winning 149 seats, the Radicals 109, and the PCF 72. Blum became the new premier of France. The causes for joy were real enough, but so was the danger.

The SFIO could not rule alone. To hold power in the Chamber of Deputies, the SFIO depended on a mistrustful communist movement that refused to participate in the ruling cabinet. Blum also depended upon support from a fundamentally anti-socialist Radical party to remain in office. In addition, the Popular Front was faced with a powerful conservative and viciously anti-Semitic fascist opposition that essentially wanted to abolish French democracy.

This situation defined the tragedy of the Popular Front. Under the circumstances, Blum could not transform the exercise of power into the conquest of power. As the Popular Front hovered between the two, each party in the original coalition sought to

UPI/BETTMANN NEWSPHOTOS

Blum emerging from a cabinet meeting in June 1936. While pursuing domestic reforms, Blum was faced with France's defense as the European situation became dangerously heated. It was an awkward period, as the socialist government was forced to prepare for war.

Blum with other members of the national council of the SFIO in 1936. Having dominated the elections of May 1936, Blum's party was ready to create a socialist government. The council was held to present the new government's plans and to draw popular support for its projected policies.

Demonstrators in Vincennes strike for higher wages. The French laborers' discontent with their working conditions was one of the main forces behind the rise of the Popular Front.

pursue its own agenda. This was true with regard to the Popular Front's economic program, political goals, and sense of purpose in foreign affairs. Indeed, the conflicts over each left the new premier to choose among the most difficult options.

The economic scene was defined by the world depression of 1929. The effects were devastating. As in all such cases, however, workers bore the brunt of the burden. Still, industrialists and businessmen were desperate to protect what profits they had previously acquired. Thus, they discharged employees by the thousands, and wages fell.

The mood among workers was dangerous. Strikes were creating panic among the financial and industrial community. Fearful of the fascists and their violent methods, the capitalists looked with dismay at the growth of revolutionary sentiments on the left. Supporting moderate elements within the Popular Front therefore became a rational choice for liberal capitalists. After all, Blum himself had said that calm was necessary to fulfill the Popular Front program.

Perhaps the Popular Front would try to institute

some economic reforms. Still, the capitalists knew that the conservative Senate would come to their aid if things got out of hand. In addition, the Radical party could always threaten to pull out of the coalition and topple the government. Indeed, far better than the SFIO, the Radicals understood that the Popular Front coalition could not last forever.

But Blum was no fool. He played upon the fears of capitalists and the excitement that the Popular Front victory had fostered. Indeed, the legislative successes the Popular Front achieved over the next weeks and months were remarkable.

The Matignon Agreement was hammered out in Blum's office residence at a hotel of the same name. By virtue of this settlement, French workers received the legal right to form unions that could demand collective contracts regarding work conditions and wages. Workers also received wage hikes of up to 15 percent, a guarantee that no reprisals would be taken against strikers, and a promise of cooperation by capitalists in implementing the Popular Front program.

Soon enough, Blum added to those achievements. Legislation was passed that created a system of pub-

> *A political phenomenon like the Popular Front does not spring up like a mushroom between the first ballot one Sunday and the runoff ballot the next.*
> —LÉON BLUM

Strikers celebrating the Popular Front victory in the national elections. Before the election, France had been paralyzed with strikes. Once in power, Blum promised a calm atmosphere while he instituted reforms. The capitalist community went along, fearful of a new wave of crippling unrest.

KEYSTONE

Upon taking office, Blum's government had immediate and extraordinary success in pressing through labor reforms. Here a group of women frolic on the beach, enjoying one of Blum's great achievements — the first paid vacations for French workers.

No government can remain stable in an unstable society and an unstable world.
—LÉON BLUM

lic works, reformed the Bank of France, nationalized the armaments industry, and extended state control over the marketing of grain. The 40-hour work week was introduced, and, to Blum's personal delight, for the first time workers were given two-week paid vacations.

Amazed at the extent of the reforms their own coalition had helped bring about, liberal capitalists now feared for their profits. They were frightened by the costs of this legislation. The Radical party therefore refused to consider further reforms. Instead, capitalists asked a high price for their support of the Matignon Agreement. They demanded compulsory arbitration of labor disputes, in ways that were basically favorable to employers. They wanted a devaluation of the French currency, which would clearly hurt workers on fixed wages, since money would be worth less. To put pressure on the SFIO, major capitalist enterprises began exporting their capital abroad and refusing to engage in domestic investment. Those tactics, which amounted to blackmail, increased unemployment and further undermined the currency.

Given all this, the Matignon Agreement was not greeted with universal celebration by the working class. The workers grumbled at the devaluation of the franc. They wondered why only one bank had been subjected to state control, and bitterly resented the fact that private control over investment remained intact. Where was that "reform of the structure" Blum had promised? Indeed, large segments of the working class felt that the reforms, which had been given with one hand, had now been taken away with the other.

Strikes continued. Workers staged sit-ins and occupied factories. Sadly, Blum learned that radical enthusiasm cannot be turned on and off like a water faucet. The idea of a popular front had made thousands of workers desire a truly revolutionary change in the political and economic system. Far more than the SFIO, these workers wanted to transform the exercise of power into the conquest of power.

This left the SFIO in an extremely difficult situation. On the one hand, the party of Jaurès was committed to parliamentary democracy and legal politics — which meant compromise with the Radicals and their capitalist supporters. On the other hand, the SFIO was traditionally committed to the working class — many of whom, with communist backing, had now taken to the streets. The conflict was clear.

The communists sought to use this situation to their advantage. Refusing to actually participate in the Popular Front government, though still tacitly supporting the coalition, the communists did not have the responsibilities of power. As the strikes spread, the PCF therefore saw an opportunity to get new political support from the working class and also undermine its socialist competitor. Thus, even while in the Chamber of Deputies the communists supported attempts to stop the strikes, in the streets they fostered "revolutionary disillusionment" with the Matignon Agreement.

Of course, the SFIO could have refused any compromises with the Radicals and agreed to the totally legitimate demands of the PCF to "make the capitalists pay." But it was the Radicals, not the PCF, who were Blum's allies in power. Had the Radicals withdrawn their support, the government would have collapsed, to the delight of the Right. The only other possibility would have involved harnessing the strength of the workers and joining with the communists in a political assault on the state and its reactionary Senate.

Blum rejected the potentially revolutionary alternative. Instead, he tried to maintain the original coalition with the Radicals. In his view, the SFIO was not a revolutionary organization and he simply distrusted the communists. It was also highly questionable whether the mass of the working class desired a revolutionary undertaking. Indeed, even the communists were actually far less inclined to revolutionary action than their words indicated.

But the real issue was a different one. Letting the coalition collapse and engaging in a revolutionary assault would have subverted the basic purpose of the Popular Front: the defense of the republic. Nevertheless, this very commitment to defend re-

Charivari, an illustrated satirical magazine, mocks Blum's devaluation of the franc. When currency is devaluated, wages stay the same but the money buys less — unpopular indeed with low-income workers.

SNARK/ART RESOURCE

UPI/BETTMANN NEWSPHOTOS

Striking workers sleep inside a Renault automobile factory. Devaluation of the franc and other compromises made by the Blum coalition angered workers who had recently celebrated wage increases that were now nullified. Strikes broke out again, and at this moment of weakness the Right and far Left attacked the government for policies that they had helped impose.

publican France made Blum a prisoner with regard to policy.

Again and again he ran up against the "wall of money." Each attempt to formulate a more radical position was undercut by the Radical threat to leave the coalition. Soon the Radicals pressed their advantage. By 1937, as gold reserves fell and capital flight increased, Blum was forced to call for a pause in his program of domestic reform.

Meanwhile, as the workers expressed their frustration through strikes, the fascists also went on the offensive. They staged large rallies. They tried to disrupt the demonstrations of the working class. Every day, the most slanderous and racist editorials filled the pages of the fascist newspapers to the point where Blum's minister of the interior was driven to suicide. Violence became a fact of political life, and workers were killed by government troops.

Though the Popular Front kept the support of the broad working masses, resentment over the pause took its toll. The communists attacked Blum for engaging in bourgeois compromise. The Radicals criticized him for being too extreme. In the Chamber of Deputies, votes of confidence began to take place regularly. Particularly in the reactionary Senate, opposition to Blum's government intensified. The political instability of the Popular Front increased and seriously affected Blum's conduct of foreign affairs.

Generally speaking, the 1930s were not a period of triumph for democracy. Fascism flourished in Finland and Poland. Hitler marched into the Rhineland, the western area of Germany, which his nation had surrendered under the Treaty of Versailles. Mussolini invaded Abyssinia (present-day Ethiopia). Japan pursued an imperialist policy on the Asian continent. Austria began to move towards fascism. The German-speaking population of Czechoslovakia's Sudetenland region looked to Hitler as a savior. In addition, Stalin began a series of domestic purges whose victims ran into the millions. Nevertheless, events in Spain perhaps most captured the imagination of the world. There the leftist, democratic forces supporting the Spanish republic were in conflict with the fascists.

From the standpoint of internationalism, the defense of French democracy was connected with the antifascist struggle abroad. But, here again, disunity existed within each party of the coalition. World War I was still a recent memory. Pacifism had gained many adherents among liberals within the SFIO and even inside the communist movement. Thus, when it came to the questions of rearming France and intervening to help democratic regimes threatened by fascism, Blum was faced with opposition not only among the populace at large, but within his own party, too.

What was true in France was also the case in other countries, most notably England. Throughout the 1930s, that country was essentially ruled by conservative governments opposed to the Soviet Union and socialist experiments of any kind. The situation only grew worse in 1937 when a new administration took office. It was led by Neville Chamberlain who, championing a policy that many would see as cowardly appeasement, sought peace with the fascist dictators at any price. Indeed, this attitude proved decisive for Blum's diplomacy when the Spanish Civil War broke out in 1936.

The Spanish conflict has now become legendary. After the abolition of the Spanish monarchy in 1934, a republic was instituted. But hatred of democracy prevailed among the Church, the military, the aristocracy, and those other groups that had supported fascist movements elsewhere in Europe. Thus, in 1936, the military staged a revolt.

Monarchists, socialists, liberals, and communists rose to defend the republic. Though a split emerged between those who wished to carry out a revolution while fighting the civil war and members of the coalition who opposed that idea, the two sides were united against the fascist movement and its leader, General Francisco Franco.

The Spanish loyalists, those who supported the republic, were at an extreme economic and military disadvantage. Still, they managed to wage a valiant struggle. It was as if good and evil were now meeting on the battlefield in preparation for the next world conflict. Thus, the Spanish Civil War quickly be-

Blum in consultation during the historic 26-hour session of the Chamber of Deputies that voted for devaluation of the franc. This measure put a brake on Blum's reforms for the moment. New labor rules and vacations remained, but the cost to the workers in wage devaluation caused new discontent that had to be addressed.

General Francisco Franco, dictator of Spain after a successful military coup in 1936. Germany and Italy actively assisted Franco, while threatening war if any other nation intervened. Under pressure from its British allies, Blum's government voted for nonintervention.

came a symbol of revolutionary freedom and anti-fascist resistance that has endured to the present.

Meanwhile, fearful of a wider war, the major nations agreed to a nonintervention pact. Hitler and Mussolini, however, quickly sent economic and military aid in vast quantities to the fascist rebels in Spain. Publicly denying their involvement, the German and Italian leaders threatened war should France or England aid the loyalist cause.

Only the Soviet Union was willing to support the loyalists with military and economic aid. In contrast to the Western democracies, Stalin respected the nonintervention agreement only to the extent that the fascists did. Indeed, the Soviet Union also played a major role in recruiting international brigades of committed individual supporters from throughout the world to assist the Spanish republic.

Leading a democratic nation, however, is not the same as heading a dictatorship. It also implies different responsibilities than leading a party. Consequently, Blum was forced to consider national security, domestic opponents, and conservative allies in a very different way than did Stalin.

The rigid nonintervention policy of England was distasteful to Blum. Still, the English alliance was clearly necessary to insure the security of France, whose own army was in little better shape than it had been at the close of World War I. England, however, was committed to nonintervention and threatened severe diplomatic reprisals should France act on its own to aid the Spanish loyalists. To which other democracy should Blum have turned for support? Indeed, when considering the French premier's plight, it is useful to recall that even the administration of U.S. President Franklin Delano Roosevelt refused to sell arms to the embattled Spanish republic.

As far as the Spanish conflict was concerned, there were only two choices open to Blum. On the one hand, he could choose to act on his international responsibilities, possibly watch the Popular Front fall, and perhaps leave France isolated before two powerful fascist nations on her borders. On the other hand, he could choose to surrender his in-

UPI/BETTMANN NEWSPHOTOS

A French fascist rally of 80,000 listens to incendiary speeches against the socialist government. The fascist attacks, including political clashes, often became violent. Between the far-left communists and the Right, Blum's Popular Front had to perform a balancing act to protect its parliamentary existence.

ternationalist obligations, refuse to give support to the Spanish loyalist cause, and remain in power a little while longer.

The constraints were real enough. As usual the communists talked tough in the streets, but on the floor of the Chamber of Deputies, they opposed sending troops. For their part, the Radicals supported nonintervention and threatened to withdraw from the coalition if Blum confronted England. Indeed, there were many in his own party who refused to support a more interventionist policy on the Spanish question.

Nevertheless, as the leader of his party and the nation, Blum could have appealed for a more vigorous policy. The communists would then have been trapped by their own rhetoric. The dissidents in the SFIO would clearly not have split while their own party was in power. It is also doubtful that England would have gone so far as to break its alliance with France on any account. Fearful of starting a war, Blum did not see that Hitler was still unprepared for a full-scale battle. Indeed, like an amateur poker player, Blum was not willing to call a bluff, and his attempt to implement a policy of relaxed nonintervention satisfied no one.

This policy was merely a desperate attempt to find room to maneuver. Refusing to allow the dispatch of even volunteer troops from France, Blum closed an eye to the illegal shipment of guns and resources

The Popular Front was no more than a reflex of instinctive defense against the perils that threatened the republic and against the prolongation of the economic crisis which was crushing the working classes, the farmers, and the middle class of the country.
—LÉON BLUM

An advertisement for Action Française, an organization of intellectual radicals of the Right. Anti-Semitic and militant, Action Française was the sort of group that Blum feared and hoped to control when he agreed to a position in Chautemps's cabinet.

I loyally defended in my party, and even at mass meetings, this program of which I did not approve.

—LÉON BLUM
on his vice-premiership in
the Chautemps cabinet

to the Spanish loyalists. He constantly expressed his personal commitment to the loyalist cause and gave sanctuary to refugees. He tried to aid the regime through nongovernmental channels and sought to provide propaganda support. Nevertheless, all of this constituted a mere fraction of what could have been accomplished had the Popular Front chosen a more assertive course.

In June 1937 the strains within the coalition came to a head. As the economic crisis and political paralysis worsened, the Radicals left the coalition. Once again refusing to call for an attack upon the Senate from below, Blum resigned. The first Popular Front government fell.

A liberal government headed by Camille Chautemps replaced it, and Blum served in the new administration as vice-premier. Though Blum had consistently opposed socialist participation in a bourgeois government, two concerns led to a reversal of that position. New fascist organizations had emerged, like the Cagoulards (Hooded Men) and the CSAR (Secret Committee for Revolutionary Action), which would stage a number of terrorist activities in the latter half of 1937. Furthermore, Blum correctly feared that a government in which the SFIO did not form part of the ruling coalition would attempt to roll back the social reforms that the Popular Front had achieved.

The SFIO, however, actually had little influence, and the Chautemps government did not last long. It collapsed trying to solve the same economic problems that the Popular Front had faced. Nevertheless, Blum loyally served Chautemps as deputy premier until March 1938.

In that month, the socialist leader received another chance. Hitler had just entered Austria, and Blum tried to create a government of national unity — which would extend from the communists to the far Right. Such a government might have built a consensus to oppose the advance of Nazism. But the conservatives and the fascists refused to participate. Thus Blum put together a second Popular Front government composed of Radicals, socialists, and communists.

This time there were fewer illusions. Understanding the basic conflicts of interest between the SFIO and its Radical ally, Blum played upon the new divisions that had surfaced within the Radical camp. Recognizing the temporary character of the coalition, he acted forcefully and decisively.

By 1938 it was clear that the Spanish fascists had won the war. Any substantial aid would now come too late and simply prolong the agony. But Blum did try to take a harder line on opposing fascism. Aside from affirming France's commitment to protect Czechoslovakia from the Nazis, he tried to begin a program of rearmament that he also hoped would improve the economy. He also called for new tax legislation, old-age pensions, and family allowances for the poor.

Once again, the communists and the Radicals put pressure on Blum's government. Once again, he faced the old choices. Once again, he refused to follow a revolutionary path. Thus, Blum's second government fell on April 8, 1938, and the era of the Popular Front came to an end.

Evaluating that era's legacy is a difficult task. Blum's legislative successes were real enough on economic issues. The reforms instituted by the Popular Front created the foundations for the modern French welfare state, and perhaps even more importantly, the Popular Front's economic policy pro-

> *Our [the Popular Front's] social legislation was of such a nature as to improve the psychological and physical conditions of the worker: a shorter work day, leisure, paid vacations, the sense of a newly acquired dignity and equality.*
> —LÉON BLUM

UPI/BETTMANN NEWSPHOTOS

Premier Blum announcing the collective resignation of his Popular Front cabinet on June 28, 1937. Against his former principles, Blum agreed to serve as vice-premier in the new Radical government of Camille Chautemps. In difficult times, Blum felt it was vital that the SFIO not abandon its influence completely.

vided the working person with a dignity and a socioeconomic standing that he never had before.

The implementation of Blum's policies assumed the need to suppress attempts by the working masses to take power and transform French society. By the same token, the very extent of Blum's reforms created the conditions for the relatively quick withdrawal of Radicals from the coalition and their destruction of the Popular Front. Thus, the Popular Front's very success on the economic front ultimately led to its political collapse.

On the level of domestic politics, romantics have surely exaggerated the level of revolutionary consciousness among the broad working class. Still, decisive actions by a major party could have deepened and extended such consciousness. To be sure, Blum wished to defend the republic. But his success was mixed. Committed to civil liberties, he never turned the power of the government against the

Fighting outside Madrid, Spanish loyalists defend the capital city against Franco's rebels. To Blum's dismay, his government could offer little more than sympathy to the meager amount of aid that was going to the overwhelmed loyalists.

Right. Thus, for a time, the Popular Front saved France from fascism, though it never actually attempted to abolish the movements and conditions in which authoritarianism could thrive.

As far as foreign policy was concerned, Blum recognized the fascist threat, sought to build a national consensus, and attempted to implement a serious rearmament program. And when it came to the crucial Spanish question, the important socialist politician Jean Zay put the matter very well when he said, "We intervened enough to provide effective support to the Republicans."

Seeking to maintain his coalition at any price, Blum refused to consider the possibility that his compromises might cause the Popular Front to cease serving its original purposes. This was particularly true with regard to his Spanish policy, which clearly strengthened the fascist belief that self-interest ruled the democracies and that they

would not fight for their weaker brethren. It probably also helped lead Stalin closer to signing the notorious nonaggression pact of August 1939 with Hitler, which would unleash the Nazi armies to begin World War II.

The great successes of Blum and the Popular Front are therefore plagued by images of timidity, vacillation, and retreat. Given all this, a question remains. Why does the Popular Front call forth such passions, loyalty, and even nostalgia? The answer actually has little to do with the success or failure of this socialist experiment in government.

There is a drama to this period and a grandeur in the decisions that Blum was forced to make. The 1930s created a mandate; that decade was not a time for politics as usual. Instead, it was a time for defining values and acting upon them. In the most basic terms, the Popular Front confronted every individual with a choice between decency and barbarism.

The Popular Front was therefore ultimately more than a governing cabinet or set of policies. It was a culture with values that touched every democratic nation and every antifascist. The traces of that culture appear in films like Jean Renoir's *The Grand Illusion*, in paintings like Picasso's *Guernica*, in novels like Ignazio Silone's *Bread and Wine*, in music, in plays, and in poetry as well.

The values that such works portrayed are simple enough. The artists of the Popular Front emphasized reason, tolerance, and that great heritage with which Blum concerned himself as a youth. They spoke to solidarity among the common people and the dignity of the individual. They presented the terrible oppression with which the unseen masses lived. They expressed the desire for peace and the willingness to sacrifice in the name of antifascism and humanistic ideals. Indeed, the ideals of solidarity and hope that the Popular Front projected would only become more compelling during the dark days that followed its collapse.

Blum talks to reporters after forming his second Popular Front government, in March 1938. The new coalition was unified by the need for action against the growing German threat. It lasted only weeks before divisions arose that caused it once again to fall.

9

A Time of Troubles

The coming years would initially prove bitter for Blum. He had seen his first wife, Lise, die in 1931. Now, he would watch his second wife, Thérèse Pereyra, to whom he had been happily married for five years, die of cancer in 1938. Following the fall of France to the Nazis, Blum learned that his son Robert had been shipped to a German prison (where, as fate would have it, he shared a cell with Stalin's son). Then his brother René, to whom he was particularly devoted, was deported to the Nazi death camp at Auschwitz (from which he never returned). Finally, Blum himself began to suffer from a variety of painful illnesses.

The political mirrored the personal. After the fall of Blum's second cabinet, he witnessed the attempt to abolish everything the Popular Front had achieved. The reaction began with a new cabinet headed by the Radical leader Édouard Daladier.

In foreign affairs, the new government became famous for refusing to confront the Nazis. The Popular Front's attempts to rearm France were quickly undermined. But there was worse to come at the Munich Conference of 1938. It was there that Daladier and Great Britain's Prime Minister Neville

> *Dictatorship and war, democracy and peace, can you dare deny the inescapable connection.*
> —LÉON BLUM

After the fall of Blum's second Popular Front administration, a new government without socialist participation began to break down the reforms that had been so difficult to achieve. At the same time, war crept closer as Hitler seemed able to command English and French diplomats to retreat before his territorial ambitions.

British Prime Minister Neville Chamberlain, French Premier Édouard Daladier, Hitler, and Mussolini (left to right) at the signing of the Munich Pact in September 1938. The pact essentially made a gift of Czechoslovakia to Germany. Blum opposed the pact in print, then agreed to it in the Chamber of Deputies, a reversal he explained as the last flickering hope for peace.

German troops advancing into France. The French were hopelessly unprepared for the German *Blitzkrieg* (lightning attack). What little resistance they offered took the form of an ordered retreat, until they finally surrendered in June 1940.

Chamberlain sacrificed Czechoslovakia to Hitler in exchange for the dictator's worthless promise of everlasting peace.

The domestic program of Daladier was no better. The new government extended the work week and allowed employers to fire workers for striking. The assault on civil liberties extended further. Bowing to the Right, Daladier also banned the PCF, expelled its leaders from the Chamber of Deputies, and closed down *L'Humanité*. Striving to maintain the image of a man of peace, he also attacked Blum as a warmonger. Indeed, under the regime of Daladier, France was flooded with fascist and anti-Semitic propaganda.

Blum denounced all of this in speeches and in print. But communist bosses like Maurice Thorez still attacked him unmercifully, and Blum's influence within his own party declined.

A great debate had begun within the SFIO. In opposition to Daladier, Blum called upon the government to confront the dictators, further rearm France, and begin military conscription. Some of Blum's followers, however, simply wished to avoid another war at any price. Others began to adapt themselves to the change in political climate. The danger of a split in the SFIO loomed large, for not many were willing to pursue policies that ran the risk of war.

But war came anyway. On September 1, 1939,

Hitler attacked Poland. The months that followed, from the autumn of 1939 into the spring of 1940, came to be known as the "phony war." War had been declared, but fighting between France and Germany had not yet begun. During that time, Paul Reynaud replaced Daladier as France's premier. Under his regime, as censorship and attacks on civil liberties increased, things only grew worse for Blum and the SFIO.

It was a demoralizing state of affairs. Fascist sentiments were running high in France. The Left was in total disarray. For Blum, the only spark of joy came from his new attachment to a devoted friend, Janot, who would share all his troubles. Indeed, she would even choose to join him in a German concentration camp—and there become his third wife.

Still, as the phony war continued, barely a day passed without some new humiliation. Fascist newspapers frankly called for Blum's assassination. Nursery rhymes with the same message were sung by schoolchildren about the hated Jewish warmonger and traitor. Fools maintained that Blum only opposed Hitler out of loyalty to his race or claimed that he wanted to sacrifice France to the dark goals of the "Jewish syndicate." Some even insisted that he was not really French at all. A privately printed brochure even asserted that Blum was really a Bulgarian national and a traitor to both countries.

But all this was only a hint of what would follow the defeat of June 1940. Through a strange series of adventures, Blum wound up staying in France, where Hitler set up a puppet regime. This new Vichy government, as it was known, was inspired by Pierre Laval and led by Marshal Philippe Pétain, the reactionary hero of World War I.

Though much has been said about the French resistance to fascism, the new dictatorship did receive a certain mass support. Blum was not surprised at the support, but it hurt the socialist leader deeply to see many former friends and Popular Front officials participate in the Vichy regime. Despite his calls for resistance, a spirit of resignation and defeat had become dominant. Indeed, all except a handful of friends deserted Blum.

Nazi soldiers enjoy a victor's holiday in Paris in 1940. The installment of the Nazi-supported Vichy government under Marshal Henri Philippe Pétain marked the end of the French republic. Soon, Blum and other socialist leaders were arrested, and "nazification" began.

Once in power, the Vichy regime started what has been called "the enterprise of Nazification." The SFIO was dissolved. For Blum, the work of a lifetime lay in ruins. Then began widespread deportation of Jews and antifascist exiles from Germany and other countries. Political arrests became routine. France became a police state.

Blum was arrested on September 15, 1940. But his case was clearly special. It was not enough to quietly ship him to a German concentration camp. It was first necessary to destroy the symbol of the Popular Front and French democracy. Thus, along with a host of other prewar leaders, including Édouard Daladier, Blum found himself on trial for political acts that allegedly compromised French readiness for war, ultimately causing the French defeat.

While in jail awaiting trial, Blum wrote an important work entitled *For All Mankind*. In that book he affirmed his old beliefs. He also tried to analyze the mistakes of the past and provide a new vision

Pétain visits Toulon in 1940. The collaboration of the Vichy government with Nazi Germany greatly embarrassed France after the war. At one point French forces were directly fighting their British allies, and when the Allied forces landed in Normandy to liberate France in 1944, some of the first opposition they encountered came from French soldiers.

General Charles de Gaulle, leader of the Free French government in exile, aboard a French destroyer based in England. De Gaulle broadcast radio messages into France calling for underground resistance. After Vichy fell, he led the Free French into the country and emerged from the war as France's greatest hero.

for the future. He still maintained that socialism could not exist without democracy and that it was necessary to abolish all forms of class exploitation. But he also criticized the working class for its disunity in the face of fascism. In the future, he maintained, socialists would have to learn to compromise and to take on national responsibilities. Finally, he insisted that the coming peace would only last if an international organization of republican states was established. Thus, his book forwarded a new vision based on the old commitment to democracy, socialism, and internationalism.

Time passed slowly in jail. Blum prepared his defense and wrote his memoirs of the phony-war period. It was in February 1942, almost a year and a

A Russian slave laborer liberated from the Buchenwald concentration camp in 1945 points an accusing finger at a Nazi guard. In history's greatest atrocity, over 6 million Jews were exterminated in camps like Buchenwald. Blum was kept alive because the Nazis shrewdly recognized his value as a hostage.

half after his arrest, that his trial began at Riom.

The charges themselves were muddled. Because he had refused to end the wave of strikes during the mid-1930s, Blum was supposed to have demoralized France. By his introducing the forty-hour work week and paid vacations and nationalizing the armaments industry the prosecution claimed that Blum had caused a major decline in production, and so left the country unprepared for war. Though it was never put quite this bluntly, the charges added up to treason.

There was no chance for a fair trial. Aside from all the legal irregularities, Marshal Pétain had already publicly pronounced the defendants guilty in advance. Nevertheless, the proceedings began.

Édouard Daladier made a fine speech. And then Blum took the podium. What remains perhaps his greatest public performance took four hours. As far as the strikers were concerned, Blum said that his principal concern was to avoid bloodshed and preserve national unity. Then he eloquently defended the Popular Front and its economic policies. Finally, however, he argued that the legal attack on his policies was really an attack on the system of majority rule, the basis of French democracy. According to Blum, it was therefore France itself that the prosecutors wished to condemn.

The Blum trial turned into a scandal. Reporters from throughout the world criticized the proceedings and compared Blum to Dreyfus. Students secretly typed up the speeches. Through underground channels, copies made their way across France and were even published abroad in a collection called *History Will Judge*. Soon enough, Léon Blum had become a symbol of democracy for the entire free world.

In Berlin, the Nazi leadership was furious. The trial was suspended, and although no verdict was ever formally given, Blum was returned to jail. Then, in March 1943, he was transferred to the notorious Buchenwald concentration camp. There he spent the next two years enduring the most incredible hardships. Given his advanced age and poor health, it was a miracle that he survived.

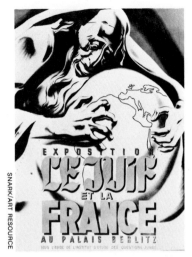

A poster promoting "The Jews and France," a Nazi propaganda exhibition spreading anti-Semitism. Nazification in France, as everywhere, featured the deportation of Jews to concentration camps — including Léon Blum, who was sent to Buchenwald, Germany, in March 1943.

At the hour when the nation awaited a clarion call, a rallying cry, no great voice could come from our ranks.
—LÉON BLUM
in his book *For All Mankind,* published in 1945

10

The Last Years

Upon his return to France, Léon Blum was greeted with a hero's welcome. Now 73 years old, France's elder statesman thought of retirement. But his party prevailed upon him. France was once again in shambles, and there was much work to be done to restore it.

A sense of national unity and enthusiasm had captured France following its liberation from the Nazis in 1945. Given their valiant record in the antifascist resistance, the socialists and particularly the communists emerged from World War II strong and confident. But the new leader of France's provisional government, General Charles de Gaulle, had little use for either. In fact, he sought a radical change from the feeble Third Republic, with its multiple parties, which had collapsed in the face of fascism.

A debate took place over the proposed character of the new French state and its constitution. De Gaulle wished to restrict the power of political parties and Parliament. Instead, he favored a political system with a strong presidency. Meanwhile, Blum feared that making the presidency too strong might

UPI/BETTMANN NEWSPHOTOS

Blum and his wife shortly after their liberation. Janot Blum had courageously chosen to go with her husband when he was imprisoned. They were released in 1945, and Blum returned to France a hero.

Blum emerged from his two-year internment in German concentration camps still committed to the cause of socialist reform. His diplomatic efforts on behalf of France's postwar socialist government helped win U.S. economic aid for his country's devastated industries.

Captured German soldiers being paraded by the French Resistance during the liberation of Paris. The Resistance was an underground army of French patriots who harassed the occupying Germans at tremendous risk. After liberation, collaborators were treated brutally as the nation sought to exorcise the shame of the war.

> *As for me, I am old, and I shall not reach the Promised Land. I shall not see the perfect union of peoples in justice and peace . . . but what marks the nobility of man is to foresee, to hope, to anticipate, to labor at work which he will not gaze on completed and from which he will not himself profit.*
> —LÉON BLUM
> speaking in New York,
> April 12, 1946

endanger democracy. He also felt that the time had come to abolish the old reactionary Senate, which had given him so much trouble during the Popular Front era. Thus, in contrast to General de Gaulle, Blum wanted to place as much power as possible in the parliamentary assembly and the political parties of France.

A compromise was finally reached. A new constitution was ratified in which the powers of the presidency were balanced by a strong National Assembly in Parliament, while the Senate was retained to check the more democratic institution. That compromise, however, was the product of a heated battle. At one point, General de Gaulle even resigned in protest, and this led to the brief reign of a socialist-led government.

It was as a representative of this socialist government that Blum traveled to the United States. Greeted with much fanfare, he successfully pleaded the case for economic assistance to his devastated nation. The result was the Blum-Byrnes Agreement of May 1946, in which the United States reduced her ally's old war debts and granted new economic credits.

Upon Blum's return, a new challenge presented itself. Between the fight over the new constitution and the overwhelming economic problems caused by the war, it was impossible to form a new government. It was as if none of the parties could agree to work together or take responsibility for the unpopular measures the situation might demand.

Political life came to a standstill. It was then that the president of the National Assembly, an old friend and colleague of Blum named Vincent Auriol, asked him to form a temporary government. The new cabinet would hold power for about five weeks until presidential elections took place in January 1947.

Blum agreed. But no other major party was willing to participate in the new government. Consequently, though the SFIO was only a minority in the parliamentary assembly, it wound up holding all the important positions in the government and therefore had to take full responsibility for all governmental measures.

Things started out badly. Two days after taking office, a revolt broke out in the French colony of Vietnam in Southeast Asia. Blum had previously expressed support for the independence of all French colonies. But since he was only heading a temporary government, granting independence to Vietnam was politically impossible. Nevertheless, as the leader of France, it was still Blum's responsibility to maintain order in its territories.

The criticisms began. Socialists were supporting imperialism! Socialists opposed the struggles for national liberation by oppressed peoples! No less than during the Spanish Civil War, Blum was condemned for his foreign policy.

This time, however, Blum did develop a broader general strategy. The "cold war" between the United States and the Soviet Union had broken out. Europe was caught in the middle as tensions mounted on both sides. Fearing a new global conflict, Blum became a proponent of Europe as an independent "Third Force" that would stand between the superpowers in an effort to negotiate peace.

Such a policy, however, clearly suggested the need to construct a European community of nations. This community would be bound economically and politically within a democratic framework. Thus, Blum wished "to create Europe while thinking of the world."

In this vein, Blum became a major advocate of the new United Nations and tried to extend its political powers. In 1945 he headed the French delegation

UPI/BETTMANN NEWSPHOTOS

Blum testifying at the trial of Marshal Pétain. The heads of the Vichy government, Pétain and Laval, were both sentenced to death. Blum spoke eloquently for a verdict of treason, though he appealed for mercy. Pétain's sentence was commuted to life imprisonment, but despite Blum's appeal to de Gaulle, Laval was executed.

to the meetings of UNESCO, an organization designed to further educational and cultural exchanges among all nations. It was fitting that Blum became its first president.

Though he would later serve for a month as vice-premier, Blum's political life really ended with the resignation of his temporary government on January 17, 1947. Its domestic record was marked by vigorous action on many fronts at once. On the economic plane, Blum lowered the prices of goods and held wages stable. In addition, he embraced the Monnet Plan, which led to increases in production over the next four years. And as the aid he had secured from the United States began to enter France, a genuine program of economic recovery emerged.

In pursuing his program and political obligations, Blum was not blind to the costs. The socialist movement was now open to criticism from every shade of the political spectrum. A strong PCF attacked him for his Vietnam policy as well as for supporting the United States' program for European recovery, called the Marshall Plan, and for refusing to give wage increases to workers.

Meanwhile, the followers of General de Gaulle were viciously attacking the institutions of France's new Fourth Republic and identifying them with Blum's party. Once again, democracy appeared to be in danger. The socialists committed themselves to maintaining the institutions of the new republic. This gave the movement a somewhat conservative image. In fact, many socialists came to the conclusion that their party was simply administering capitalist policy. The socialist movement's sense of purpose started to slip away, along with its voters.

Divisions appeared within the party itself. Some wanted to revive the militant spirit of the old SFIO. Others basically accepted the approach Blum had outlined in *For All Mankind*. Many of those in the former group gradually left the SFIO and entered the communist movement. Many in the latter group abandoned the SFIO for more liberal parties.

The party started to shrink. Before the war, the existence of the Third Republic had depended upon

Blum, French Ambassador Henri Bonnet, U.S. Secretary of State James Byrnes, and Secretary of the Treasury Fred Vinson (right to left) at the signing of the loan agreement with the United States for the rebuilding of France. Blum had gone to the meeting as a representative of France, and upon his return was asked to form one more government, to reign briefly until presidential elections could be held.

a strong socialist movement. Now, it was as if the preservation of the new Fourth Republic demanded the sacrifice of the socialist movement.

Blum was willing to pay the price. Though more than a simple reformist, he was never a revolutionary. It was always dictatorship, whether of the Right or the Left, that was the enemy. Thus, whatever the changes in Blum's thinking, he remained loyal to his original conviction that a democratic political order was the precondition for socialist activity.

Blum would never see the great transformation to a socialist order. But through his work, new steps were taken in that direction. Through his policies, workers received basic political rights that would protect them economically.

Nevertheless, the welfare state remains a type of capitalism. Reforms are still only possible if their costs do not greatly threaten the profits of the capitalist class. Investment remains in private hands. It is still much easier for the rich than for the poor to get together over issues, gain access to information, and raise funds for political purposes. Whatever the advances, welfare capitalism still provides greater privileges for the wealthy.

Abolishing those conditions democratically is still the purpose of that notion of socialism to which Léon Blum dedicated his life. But perhaps he was a bit too naive. In a way, he never really learned the lesson of the Popular Front. Blum continued to be-

"The example of Léon Blum," wrote novelist François Mauriac, "reminds us that ennoblement is possible and that, despite all defeats, life is a contest which, until the end, we are free to win."

lieve that social reforms could please everyone. Until his death, he assumed that goodwill would overcome the conflicting political and economic interests of different classes.

Still, Blum remains a symbol. Always open to debate, both his theoretical and practical activities were defined by an intellectual clarity as well as a sense of ethical purpose. Indeed, Blum showed that an intellectual, and one with strong moral principles, could enter politics.

Some have suggested that these very qualities hindered him as a politician. His intellectual level and his sense of justice are sometimes seen as the cause of what some consider his mistakes and lack of decisiveness. But this is a poor argument. In different ways, both Lenin and de Gaulle were also intellectuals with a sense of justice and purpose. What separated them from Blum was his particular political commitment.

History allows no politician to do what he pleases. Alternatives are always defined by the constraints of context. Blum was not responsible for the existence of French fascism, the rise of Stalinism, or the opposition of a calculating Radical party. These were the constraints on his freedom to act.

A judgment on his career depends upon recognizing that it was necessary for Blum to balance his commitments to socialism, democracy, and internationalism. Blum may have made mistakes and exhibited a lack of revolutionary daring, but this was not because he was an intellectual or because he was concerned with abstract matters of justice. Instead, the crucial factor is that Blum was a democrat. Indeed, he ultimately acted no differently than the best European socialist leaders of his generation who found themselves in similar circumstances during the 1920s and 1930s.

What separated Blum from many others, however, was his abiding belief that socialism was more than reforms and more than any set of institutions. Beyond commitment to his particular choices or tactics, this is where Blum's legacy lies. He saw socialism as an ongoing attempt to improve the living condition of working people, to build a new culture with more humane economic values, to overcome apathy and exploitation, to break down old barriers that separate people, and to further democratic participation at all levels of society.

Léon Blum died of a heart attack on March 30, 1950, shortly before his 78th birthday. As his eyes closed, he must have reflected on the many contributions he had made to the struggle for freedom. Thinking of what he had endured and achieved, he must have recognized how little he had missed in his long life. Death must have become just another enemy. Blum's last words to his wife, Janot, therefore made perfect sense: "It is nothing, do not be afraid for me."

Parisians line the streets in April 1950 to pay their last respects to Léon Blum. The casket rested in the lobby of the socialist newspaper *Le Populaire*. In a fitting symbol for a socialist, the funeral procession was led by hundreds of miners with the lamps on their mining helmets lit.

Further Reading

Blum, Léon. *For All Mankind,* tr. W. Pickles. Magnolia, Massachusetts: Peter Smith Publishers, 1979.

———. *Marriage,* tr. Warre B. Wells. New York: AMS Press, Inc., 1975.

Colton, Joel. *Léon Blum: Humanist in Politics.* New York: Alfred A. Knopf, Inc., 1966.

Dalby, Louise Elliott. *Léon Blum: Evolution of a Socialist.* New York: Thomas Yoseloff, 1963.

Goldberg, Harvey. *The Life of Jean Jaurès.* Madison, Wisconsin: University of Wisconsin Press, 1962.

Joll, James. *Intellectuals in Politics: Three Biographical Essays* (Blum, Rathenau, and Marinetti). New York: Harper & Row, 1960.

———. *The Second International 1889–1914.* New York: Harper & Row, 1966.

Lacouture, Jean. *Léon Blum,* tr. George Holoch. New York: Holmes & Meier, 1982.

Lewis, David L. *Prisoners of Honor: The Dreyfus Affair.* New York: William Morrow & Co., Inc., 1973.

Lichtheim, George. *Marxism: An Historical and Critical Study.* New York: Frederick A. Praeger, 1961.

Logue, William. *Léon Blum: The Formative Years, 1872–1914.* DeKalb, Illinois: Northern Illinois University Press, 1973.

Chronology

April 9, 1872	Born André-Léon Blum in Paris
1894	Receives law degree from the Sorbonne
1895–1919	Serves as an attorney for the French government
1896	The revelation that French captain Alfred Dreyfus has been wrongfully convicted by the army of selling military secrets to Germany precipitates a national crisis
1899	Blum joins a socialist organization, Socialist Unity
1901	Publishes *New Conversations of Goethe with Eckermann*, a series of philosophical, literary, and political essays
April 1905	Disparate socialist groups agree to form a single party and adopt the name the French Section of the Labor International (SFIO)
1905–14	Blum withdraws from politics to pursue his legal work and his career as a literary and drama critic
July 31, 1914	French socialist leader Jean Jaurès is assassinated
1914–16	Blum receives his first governmental appointment as an aide to the minister of public works, Marcel Sembat
Nov. 1917	The Bolshevik party seizes power in the Russian Revolution
March 1919	Bolshevik leader V. I. Lenin forms the Third International to coordinate a global network of communist parties
Nov. 1919	Blum is elected to the Chamber of Deputies
1919	Blum becomes leader of the SFIO
Dec. 1920	A dissident faction breaks from the SFIO at a party congress in Tours and forms the French Communist party (PCF)
1926	Blum introduces his distinction between the "exercise" and the "conquest" of power at the Bellevilloise Socialist congress
July 14, 1935	Communists, socialists and middle-class liberals agree to form a ".popular front" in the wake of vicious profascist riots
June 1936	Blum becomes the first Jew and the first Socialist to serve as premier of France after the Popular Front wins a majority in the Chamber of Deputies
1936–37	Wins passage of numerous bills benefitting French workers
June 1937	Resigns as premier after losing the support of the Radical party A new government is formed under Camille Chautemps, who appoints Blum as vice-premier
March–Apr., 1938	Blum's second Popular Front administration
Sept. 15, 1940	Blum is arrested by the Vichy government of France
Feb. 1942	Brought to trial in Riom
1943–45	Interned in Buchenwald, a Nazi concentration camp
1946–47	Heads a provisional government that implements plans to revive France's war-ravaged economy
Dec. 18, 1946	A war of independence breaks out in Vietnam
March 30, 1950	Blum dies, aged 77, of a heart attack, at Jouy-en-Josas

Index

Stephen Bronner is Associate Professor of Political
Science at Rutgers University. He received his B.A.
from the City College of New York and his Ph.D. from
the University of California at Berkeley. A contributor
to many scholarly publications, Bronner has edited
and written several books in the fields of history and
political science.

Arthur M. Schlesinger, jr., taught history at Harvard
for many years and is currently Albert Schweitzer Professor of the Humanities at City University of New
York. He is the author of numerous highly praised
works in American history and has twice been
awarded the Pulitzer Prize. He served in the White
House as special assistant to Presidents Kennedy and
Johnson.